Letts

CAMBRIDGE IGCSE® BIOLOGY

Revision Guide

Mary Jones

ACKNOWLEDGEMENTS

Cover photo © Noppharat4569 / Alamy Stock Photo
Illustrations by Greenhill Wood Studios, Banbury, UK
Original illustrations on pages 30, 32, 40 bottom, 45, 51, 52 top, 53, 61, 66 middle and bottom, 68, 83, 112, 117
by Jouve India Private Ltd, and Ann Paganuzzi

Every effort has been made to trace copyright holders and obtain their permission for the use of copyright
material. The author and publisher will gladly receive information enabling them to rectify any error or
omission in subsequent editions. All facts are correct at time of going to press.

Published by Letts Educational
An imprint of HarperCollins*Publishers*
The News Building
1 London Bridge Street
London
SE1 9GF

ISBN 978-0-00-821031-1

First published 2017

10 9 8 7 6 5 4 3 2 1

© HarperCollins*Publishers* Limited 2017

® IGCSE is the registered trademark of Cambridge International Examinations.
Exam-style practice questions and sample answers have been written by the author.

Mary Jones asserts her moral right to be identified as the author of this work.

British Library Cataloguing in Publication Data
A CIP record for this book is available from the British Library.

Commissioned by Katherine Wilkinson
Project managed by Kate Ellis, Sheena Shanks
Edited by Helen Bleck
Proofread by Jess White
Cover design by Paul Oates
Typesetting by Green Hill Wood Studios, Banbury, UK
Production by Natalia Rebow, Lyndsey Rogers and Paul Harding
Printed and bound in Great Britain by Martins the Printers

FSC™ is a non-profit international organisation established to promote the
responsible management of the world's forests. Products carrying the FSC
label are independently certified to assure consumers that they come from
forests that are managed to meet the social, economic and ecological needs
of present and future generations, and other controlled sources.

Find out more about HarperCollins and the environment at
www.harpercollins.co.uk/green

Contents

Chapter 5 Coordination

Chapter 6 Reproduction

Chapter 7 Genetics and selection

Chapter 8 Organisms and environment

Answers

Glossary

Introduction

This revision guide will help you to prepare for your Cambridge IGCSE® Biology examinations. It covers all of the learning objectives in the Biology syllabus.

The guide is divided into eight chapters. Each chapter covers several sections of the syllabus.

The main text describes and explains the learning objectives from the Core syllabus. Supplement material is shown on a blue background. Diagrams are often used instead of, or as well as, text.

This syllabus contains many definitions, which you should learn by heart, and these are all shown in boxes with a blue outline. The definitions are summarised in the Glossary at the end of the book.

You will find Revision tips on many of the pages in the guide. They explain how to avoid some very common errors that students make when they write answers to questions.

Revision is only successful if you do something active, rather than simply reading. You could try rewriting some of the material in a different form. For example, you could convert a paragraph of text into a series of bullet points, or change a set of bullet points into a table. There are sets of Quick test questions at the end of each section, which you can use to check that you have understood and remembered the content you have just worked through. The answers to these questions are at the back of the book.

At the end of each chapter, there is a set of Exam-style practice questions. These are similar to the questions on the Cambridge theory papers. Each section has a mark allocation, which you should use to help you decide how much to write in your answer, and how much detail to give. Mark schemes for these questions are also at the back of the book.

You will find a list of the contents on pages 3 to 5. You could use this to keep track of your progress as you work through the guide. Perhaps you could tick the box in one colour when you have first worked through a section, and then in another colour when you have gone over it again, and have answered all of the questions correctly.

Classification of living organisms

All living organisms have seven characteristics.

Definitions

Movement – an action by an organism or part of an organism causing a change of position or place.

Respiration – the chemical reactions in cells that break down nutrient molecules and release energy for metabolism.

Sensitivity – the ability to detect or sense stimuli in the internal or external environment and to make appropriate responses.

Growth – a permanent increase in size and dry mass by an increase in cell number or cell size or both.

Excretion – removal from organisms of the waste products of metabolism (chemical reactions in cells including respiration), toxic materials, and substances in excess of requirements.

Nutrition – taking in materials for energy, growth and development; plants require light, carbon dioxide, water and ions; animals need organic compounds and ions and usually need water.

Reproduction – making more of the same kind of organism.

Classifying species

Organisms that share similar features are classified into the same groups. The smallest group is the **species**.

Definition

Species – a group of organisms that can reproduce to produce fertile offspring.

Naming species

Groups of similar species are classified together in the same **genus**.

Each species is given an internationally agreed two-word name, called a **binomial**.

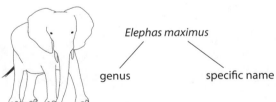

Elephas maximus

genus   specific name

Definition

Binomial system – an internationally agreed system in which the scientific name of an organism is made up of two parts showing the genus and species.

Revision tip

You should learn all definitions by heart.

Revision tip

If you are studying the Core syllabus only, there is a simpler set of definitions that you could learn instead. Ask your teacher about this.

Supplement

To classify organisms, biologists compare their:

- morphology – the overall structure of the organism
- anatomy – the more detailed structure, such as the positions and shapes of organs
- sequences of amino acids that make up proteins
- sequences of bases that make up DNA.

Each species has evolved from another species. The more similar their DNA, the more recently they shared a common ancestor, so they are more closely related to each other.

Revision tip

When writing a binomial, always use a capital letter for the first word and a small letter for the second word.

Dichotomous keys

A key is a series of questions or statements that helps you to identify an unknown organism.

In a dichotomous key, there are pairs of questions or statements. 'Di' means 'two'. Your choice from each pair leads you to another pair.

Try using this key to determine the group that this animal belongs to. Even though you have not learnt about this animal or this group, you should be able to follow the key and find that the animal is an annelid.

1a	has legs	go to 2
b	does not have legs	go to 3
2a	has six legs	insects
b	has eight legs	arachnids
3a	has segments	annelids
b	does not have segments	molluscs

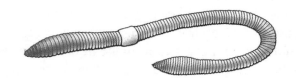

> **Revision tip**
>
> If you are asked to write your own key, remember that it should be possible for the user of the key to choose the correct statement without having to compare one organism with another.

Classification groups

The largest classification groups are called **kingdoms**.

Organisms belonging to the **animal kingdom** and the **plant kingdom** have different kinds of cells. See the diagram on page 10.

The animal kingdom includes vertebrates and arthropods.

Vertebrates have a backbone

mammals
hair, four-chambered heart, placenta, mammary glands, different types of teeth

birds
feathers, four-chambered heart, wings, beak, lay eggs with hard shells

reptiles
scales, lay soft-shelled eggs on land

amphibians
smooth skin, lay eggs with no shells in water

fish
scales, lay eggs with no shells in water

Arthropods have
• jointed legs
• segmented bodies

arachnids
body divided into head and cephalothorax, four pairs of jointed legs

insects
body divided into head, thorax and abdomen, six jointed legs attached to the thorax, four wings attached to the thorax

myriapods
many similar segments, each with at least one pair of jointed legs

crustaceans
more than four pairs of jointed legs, hard shell

> **Revision tip**
>
> Make sure that you spell arthropod correctly. It does not have an n in it.

The table shows some of the main characteristics of all of the five kingdoms.

Animal kingdom	Plant kingdom	Fungus kingdom	Protoctist kingdom	Prokaryote kingdom
• cells with no cell walls • multicellular • feed on organic substances made by other organisms	• cells with cell walls made of cellulose • multicellular • make their own organic substances from inorganic ones, by photosynthesis	• cells with cell walls not made of cellulose • multicellular or single-celled • feed on dead or decaying organic material	• single-celled organisms with a nucleus • some have cell walls and chloroplasts, and some do not	• single-celled organisms, with no nucleus, mitochondria or endoplasmic reticulum • have a cell wall, but are not made of cellulose

There are several groups within the plant kingdom. These include:

- **ferns**, which have leaves called fronds and reproduce with spores that grow on the backs of the fronds.
- **flowering plants**, which have flowers and seeds for reproduction.

Flowering plants include:

- **monocotyledons**, which have seeds containing a single cotyledon. Their flowers usually have parts in sets of three. Their leaves are often strap-shaped with parallel veins. They often have a branching root system.

- **dicotyledons**, which have seeds containing two cotyledons. Their flowers usually have parts in sets of four or five. Their leaves are often broad, with a network of veins. They often have a tap root.

Viruses are not usually classed as living organisms because they are not made of cells. A virus is a piece of genetic material (either DNA or RNA) enclosed in a protein coat.

monocotyledon

dicotyledon

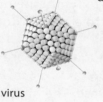
virus

Quick test

1. Write out the definitions of each of the seven characteristics of living things, without looking them up.
2. Polar bears belong to the genus *Ursus* and the species *maritimus*. Write the binomial of a polar bear.
3. List **two** differences between organisms belonging to the plant kingdom and the animal kingdom.
4. List **two** differences between amphibians and reptiles.
5. List **two** features of all arthropods.

Supplement

6. State **three** features of species that biologists use to decide how closely they are related.
7. An organism is made of single cells, each with a chloroplast and a cell wall made of cellulose. What kingdom does it belong to?
8. A plant has flowers, leaves with a network of veins and a tap root. Name **two** groups that this plant belongs to.

Cells, tissues and organs

The diagrams show a typical animal cell and a typical plant cell.

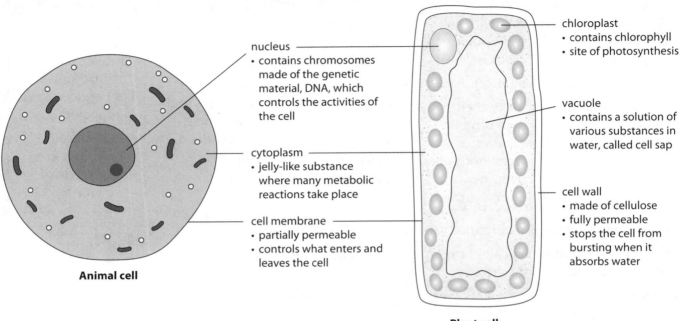

nucleus
• contains chromosomes made of the genetic material, DNA, which controls the activities of the cell

cytoplasm
• jelly-like substance where many metabolic reactions take place

cell membrane
• partially permeable
• controls what enters and leaves the cell

Animal cell

chloroplast
• contains chlorophyll
• site of photosynthesis

vacuole
• contains a solution of various substances in water, called cell sap

cell wall
• made of cellulose
• fully permeable
• stops the cell from bursting when it absorbs water

Plant cell

Supplement

Almost all cells (except prokaryotes) also contain:

• **ribosomes.** These are tiny structures where amino acids are linked together to synthesise proteins. Many of the ribosomes in a cell are attached to a network of membranes called the rough endoplasmic reticulum.
• **mitochondria.** These are sausage-shaped structures where aerobic respiration takes place. Aerobic respiration releases useful energy from glucose. The higher the rate of metabolism a cell has, the more energy it needs and the more mitochondria it has.
• **vesicles.** These are tiny fluid-filled sacs in the cytoplasm, surrounded by a membrane.

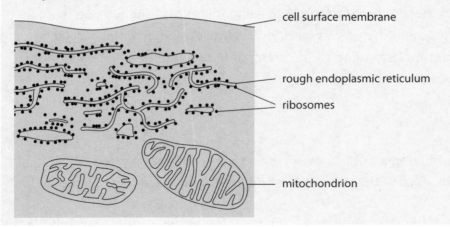

cell surface membrane

rough endoplasmic reticulum

ribosomes

mitochondrion

> ### Revision tip
>
> Notice that the cell wall is thick and is shown as a double line. The cell membrane is very thin, and is pressed up so tight against the inside of the cell wall that it cannot be seen as a separate structure.

In a multicellular organism, each cell is specialised for a particular function. For example:

In mammals:

- ciliated cells help to move mucus up the trachea and bronchi;
- red blood cells transport oxygen;
- sperm and egg cells are gametes involved in sexual reproduction;
- nerve cells (neurones) transmit information in the form of electrical impulses.

In flowering plants:

- root hair cells absorb water from the soil;
- xylem vessels transport water and provide support;
- palisade mesophyll cells in leaves carry out photosynthesis.

You can find diagrams of each of these cells in the sections of this book where their functions are described.

Cells that carry out the same function are often found together, forming a **tissue**, for example muscle tissue.

Groups of tissues form **organs**, for example the heart.

Groups of organs form **organ systems**, for example the circulatory system.

Definitions

Tissue – a group of cells with similar structures, working together to perform a shared function.
Organ – a structure made up of a group of tissues, working together to perform specific functions.
Organ system – a group of organs with related functions working together to perform body functions.

Magnification

Cells are very small, so we often use magnified images of cells.

$$\text{magnification} = \frac{\text{size of image}}{\text{real size}}$$

$$\text{real size} = \frac{\text{size of image}}{\text{magnification}}$$

For example, if we know that the diagram of the animal cell on the previous page has a magnification of × 1500, then we can calculate its real size like this:

diameter of the cell in the image = 57 mm

$$\text{so real size} = \frac{57\,\text{mm}}{1500} = 0.038\,\text{mm}$$

Supplement

Micrometres, μm, are useful when dealing with very small things.
1 μm = 10^{-3} mm or 10^{-6} m.

Revision tip

Magnification does not have units. Write the magnification simply as a × sign and a number.

Revision tip

When you are doing magnification calculations, begin by converting all measurements to the same units. These could be mm or μm.

Quick test

1. List **three** structures found in all animal cells and all plant cells.
2. Outline the function of each of the structures in your answer to 1.
3. What is the function of red blood cells?
4. What is the function of palisade cells?
5. Write down the definition of a tissue.
6. A diagram of a leaf is 120 mm long. The real leaf is 40 mm long. What is the magnification of the diagram?

Supplement

7. Which types of cells contain mitochondria?
8. What is the function of mitochondria?
9. Which types of cells contain ribosomes?
10. What is the function of ribosomes?
11. A micrograph of a chloroplast shows it is 20 mm long. The magnification of the micrograph is ×2000. Calculate the actual length of the chloroplast. Give your answer in μm.

Diffusion, osmosis and active transport

Diffusion

All substances are made up of unimaginably small particles in constant motion. In gases and liquids, including solutions, these particles move around quite freely. In solids, the particles vibrate in one place.

If a solute is in a higher concentration in one area of a solution than another, we say there is a **concentration gradient** for the solute. The random motion of its particles causes them to eventually spread out evenly. This also happens in gases. This is **diffusion**.

> ### Definition
>
> **Diffusion** – the net movement of particles from a region of their higher concentration to a lower concentration down a concentration gradient, as a result of their random movement.

> **Revision tip**
>
> You can think of a concentration gradient as a 'slope' from the higher concentration to the lower concentration. Diffusion results in net movement down the slope.

> **Revision tip**
>
> 'Net' means 'overall'. Particles move randomly in both directions, but more of them move from the area of higher concentration to the area of lower concentration than in the other direction.

> **Supplement**
>
> The energy for the movement of particles in diffusion comes from the kinetic energy of the particles themselves. The higher the temperature, the greater this kinetic energy. Diffusion therefore takes place faster at higher temperatures.

Many substances diffuse into and out of living cells. For example, in a respiring cell, oxygen dissolved in the cytoplasm is constantly being used up. This produces a low concentration of oxygen inside the cell. There is likely to be a higher concentration of oxygen outside the cell. Oxygen therefore diffuses down its concentration gradient into the cell, through the cell membrane.

> **Supplement**
>
> You can use agar jelly to investigate the factors that influence diffusion. You can make agar jelly that contains a small quantity of acid and some Universal Indicator, so that the jelly is red.
>
> For example, to investigate how surface area affects the rate of diffusion, cut the jelly into shapes with different surface areas but the same mass and volume. Place the shapes into a dilute solution of sodium carbonate. As the sodium carbonate diffuses into the jelly, it neutralises the acid in the jelly and the colour changes from red to blue or green. You can measure the rate of diffusion by recording the time it takes for the whole piece of jelly to change colour.
>
> This technique can also be used to investigate how temperature, concentration gradient and distance affect the rate of diffusion of the sodium carbonate into the jelly. In each case, you should change the variable you are investigating, and keep all other variables constant.

Osmosis

Osmosis is a special kind of diffusion. Osmosis is the diffusion of water through a membrane that allows water molecules to pass through, but does not allow other particles through. This kind of membrane is called a **partially permeable membrane**.

Examples of partially permeable membranes include:

- cell membranes
- Visking tubing.

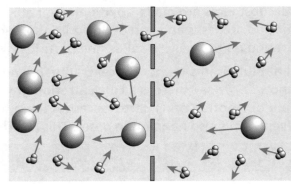

concentrated sugar solution   dilute sugar solution

holes allow water molecules to pass through

sugar molecules and water molecules move randomly

partially permeable membrane

net movement of the water molecules is from the dilute solution to the concentrated solution

Supplement

We do not normally talk about the 'concentration' of water. Instead, we use the term water potential. The more water there is in a solution, the higher its **water potential**. Water molecules therefore diffuse from a solution with a high water potential to a solution with a lower water potential, down a water potential gradient.

Definition

Osmosis – the net movement of water molecules from a region of higher water potential (dilute solution) to a region of lower water potential (concentrated solution) through a partially permeable membrane.

Osmosis and cells

You can investigate how osmosis affects plant tissues using cylinders cut from potato tubers.

Measure the mass or length of the cylinders. Then place them into solutions of salt or sugar of different concentrations. Leave them for about 20 minutes. Then take them out and measure the mass or length of each one again. Calculate the change in mass or length, making sure that you state whether it is an increase or decrease. You can then draw a line graph with concentration of the solution on the *x*-axis and change in mass or length on the *y*-axis.

Pieces of potato tuber placed in pure water or solutions that are more dilute than the cell contents will take up water by osmosis, and will increase in length and mass. They become firm and strong, because the extra water inside the cells presses outwards on the cell walls. This is an important way in which plant tissues are supported.

If the solutions are more concentrated than the cell contents, then the potato will lose water by osmosis and will decrease in length or mass.

 Revision tip

Remember that in osmosis it is only *water molecules* that move into or out of the cell. Do not say that the *solution* moves.

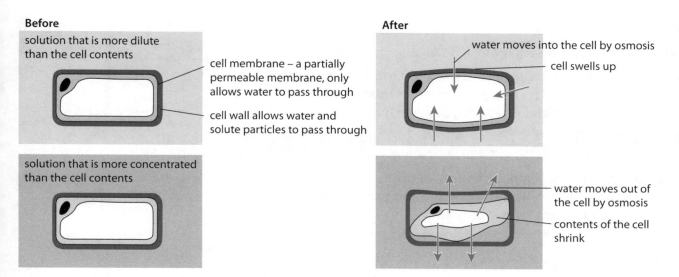

Before

solution that is more dilute than the cell contents

cell membrane – a partially permeable membrane, only allows water to pass through

cell wall allows water and solute particles to pass through

solution that is more concentrated than the cell contents

After

water moves into the cell by osmosis

cell swells up

water moves out of the cell by osmosis

contents of the cell shrink

Supplement

A cell that has taken up water by osmosis is like an inflated balloon. It is said to be **turgid**. The contents of the cell press outwards on its walls; this is called **turgor pressure**. The cell walls cannot stretch, and are said to be inelastic. The turgidity of a plant's cells helps to support the soft parts of a plant, such as its leaves and flower petals.

A cell that has lost water by osmosis is said to be **flaccid**. If it loses a large amount of water, then the cell contents shrink so much that the cell membrane pulls away from the cell wall. The cell is said to be **plasmolysed**.

cell wall is inelastic and does not cave inwards very much

contents of cell shrink as they have lost a lot of water

cell membrane has pulled away from cell wall

Plasmolysed cell

If a flaccid cell is immersed in a dilute solution, the cell will take up water by osmosis and the cell will become turgid. However, once a cell is plasmolysed, the cell membrane is often irreversibly damaged, and the cell is likely to die.

Root hair cells take up water from the soil because the water potential inside them is lower than the water potential in the soil. Water therefore moves into the root hair cell by osmosis, down a water potential gradient, through the partially permeable cell membrane.

Animal cells are also affected by osmosis and water potential. Unlike plant cells, animal cells do not have a cell wall. There is therefore nothing to stop them from bursting when they take up a lot of water by osmosis.

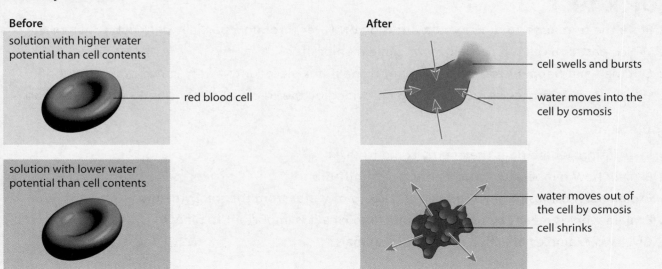

Before

solution with higher water potential than cell contents

red blood cell

solution with lower water potential than cell contents

After

cell swells and bursts

water moves into the cell by osmosis

water moves out of the cell by osmosis

cell shrinks

Active transport

In diffusion and osmosis, particles move down a concentration gradient.

Cells can make particles move *up* a concentration gradient. To do this, the cell has to provide energy. The energy is provided from respiration. This type of movement of particles is called **active transport**.

Definition

Active transport – the movement of particles through a cell membrane from a region of lower concentration to a region of higher concentration using energy from respiration.

Revision tip

Take care not to suggest that energy is 'made' by respiration. Energy cannot be made. Energy can only be changed from one form to another. In respiration, energy in glucose is changed into energy that the cell can use for various different purposes, including active transport.

Supplement

Active transport is used:

- by root hair cells of plants to move ions (for example, nitrate ions) from the soil into the root hair, when the concentration of ions in the soil is lower than the concentration in the root hair;
- by epithelial cells of the villi in the ileum of humans to move glucose from the intestine into the blood;
- by cells lining kidney tubules to move glucose from the contents of the tubule back into the blood.

Active transport is carried out by protein molecules in the cell membranes.

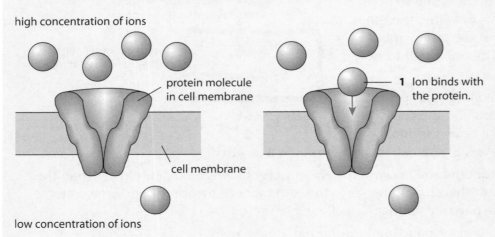
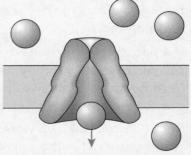

high concentration of ions

protein molecule in cell membrane

cell membrane

low concentration of ions

1 Ion binds with the protein.

2 Energy from respiration is used to make the protein change shape.

3 This moves the ion across the cell membrane.

Quick test

1. State the term used to describe the diffusion of water through a partially permeable membrane.
2. Which part of a cell is a partially permeable membrane?
3. Outline what happens to a piece of plant tissue if it is placed into a very concentrated solution.
4. Which of these processes require energy provided by the cell: diffusion, osmosis, active transport?

Supplement

5. In diffusion, where does the energy come from?
6. Explain how temperature affects the rate of diffusion.
7. Explain how osmosis is involved in the take-up of water from the soil by plants.
8. Explain what is meant by turgor pressure, and why it is important to plants.
9. Give two examples of active transport in animals.

Biological molecules

The most abundant substance in living organisms is water. Water is an important solvent.

Water acts as a solvent:

- in digestion, allowing enzymes to come into contact with nutrients in food;
- in excretion, allowing unwanted substances such as urea to be transported out of the body in urine;
- in transport, allowing many solutes to be transported in blood plasma, including urea, glucose and amino acids.

The table shows information about carbohydrates, fats and proteins. These are all organic substances.

Substance	Elements contained	Examples	Smaller molecules from which it is made	Test	Positive test result
carbohydrates	C, H, O	glucose		heat with Benedict's solution	brick-red precipitate
		starch	glucose	add iodine solution	blue-black colour
		glycogen	glucose		
		cellulose	glucose		
fats and oils	C, H, O		fatty acids glycerol	emulsion test: dissolve in ethanol then pour into water	milky appearance
proteins	C, H, O, N		amino acids	add biuret solution	purple colour

Vitamins, for example vitamin C, are also organic substances. To test for vitamin C, add DCPIP. Vitamin C causes dark blue DCPIP to become colourless.

Supplement

There are twenty different amino acids. The sequence in which they link together affects the final shape and function of the protein molecule that is formed.

For example:

- the shape of an enzyme molecule affects the shape of its active site, and this determines the substrate with which it can bind, and the reaction that it can catalyse;
- the shape of an antibody molecule affects the shape of its binding site, and this determines the specific antigen with which it can bind.

DNA

DNA is the chemical that makes up chromosomes, found in the nuclei of cells. It carries information that is transferred from parents to offspring.

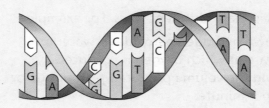

- Two strands are coiled together to form a double helix.
- Each strand is made up of a long chain of smaller molecules, each of which contains a base.
- There are cross-links between the bases – always A with T and C with G.

Enzymes

Enzymes are proteins that catalyse metabolic reactions. Without enzymes, these reactions would happen so slowly – in most cases, not at all – that life could not be sustained.

Definitions

Catalyst – a substance that increases the rate of a chemical reaction and is not changed by the reaction.
Enzyme – a protein that functions as a biological catalyst.

An enzyme has a shape that is **complementary** to the **substrate** molecules whose reaction it catalyses. The substrate molecule binds temporarily to the enzyme. The enzyme changes the substrate to **product** and then releases it. The enzyme is unchanged and can now repeat the process with another molecule of its substrate.

Revision tip

Take care not to say that an enzyme has the *same* shape as its substrate. The shapes are complementary, meaning that one is a mirror image of the other, allowing them to fit together perfectly.

Supplement

The part of the enzyme molecule that binds with the substrate molecule is known as the **active site**. Because the enzyme can only bind with substrate with a complementary shape to the active site, each enzyme is **specific** for a particular substrate.

The substrate and enzyme form a very short-lived **enzyme–substrate complex**. The substrate is converted to product and then released from the active site.

1

enzyme molecule

active site – a complementary shape to the substrate molecule

substrate molecule

2

enzyme–substrate complex

3

enzyme is unchanged

product is released

Enzymes and temperature

You can investigate the effect of temperature on an enzyme-catalysed reaction by:

- placing a standard volume of a solution of an enzyme into five different test tubes;
- placing a standard volume of a solution of the enzyme's substrate into five different test tubes;
- standing all ten test tubes in water baths at different temperatures – for example 0 °C, 20 °C, 40 °C, 60 °C, 80 °C and leaving them to come to the required temperature;
- adding the enzyme to the substrate and measuring the rate of reaction.

Rate of reaction can be measured in many different ways. For example:

- The enzyme **catalase** breaks down hydrogen peroxide to water and oxygen. You can measure the rate at which oxygen is produced by collecting the gas and measuring the volume produced per minute, or by measuring the loss of mass per minute.

- The enzyme **amylase** breaks down starch to the sugar maltose. You can measure the rate at which the starch is broken down by taking a sample from the reacting mixture every two minutes, and adding it to iodine solution on a tile to check whether it still gives a blue-black colour.

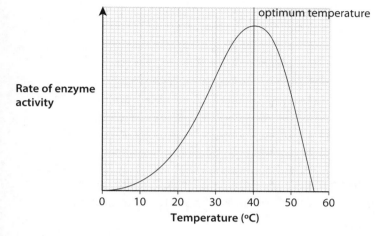

Supplement

Most chemical reactions, including those catalysed by enzymes, happen slowly at low temperatures. This is because the kinetic energy of the enzyme and substrate are low, so they move slowly and collide infrequently.

As temperature increases, kinetic energy increases and collisions become more frequent, so reaction rate increases. However, above the enzyme's optimum temperature, the enzyme molecule begins to lose its shape – it is **denatured**. The active site no longer fits the substrate, so no enzyme–substrate complexes are formed and the reaction does not take place. The enzyme cannot regain its shape now, even if the temperature falls.

Enzymes and pH

pH is a measure of the acidity of a solution. The more acidic a solution, the lower its pH. Most, but not all, enzymes work best at around pH7 (neutral).

You can investigate the effect of pH on an enzyme-catalysed reaction by:

- placing a standard volume of a solution of an enzyme into five different test tubes;
- placing a standard volume of a solution of the enzyme's substrate into five different test tubes;
- placing a standard volume of **buffer solutions** of different pHs into each tube containing the enzyme;
- standing all ten test tubes in a water bath at the enzyme's optimum temperature;
- adding the enzyme/buffer mixture to the substrate and measuring the rate of reaction.

> **Revision tip**
>
> A buffer solution is a solution that has a particular pH, and that maintains the same pH even when a chemical reaction is taking place.

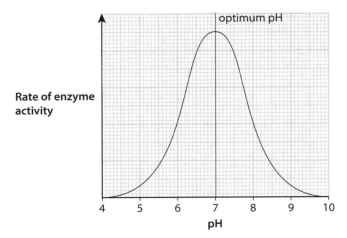

Supplement

pH affects the shape of an enzyme, and therefore the fit of its substrate into its active site. At a pH above or below its optimum, an enzyme becomes denatured and so is unable to form enzyme–substrate complexes.

Quick test

1. Name the element found in proteins that is **not** found in carbohydrates or fats.
2. Name the smaller molecules that link together to form cellulose molecules.
3. Describe how you would test a solution to find out if it contained protein.
4. What is DCPIP used for?
5. Describe why enzymes are important in all living organisms.
6. Describe how enzyme activity is affected by temperature.

Supplement

7. Outline **two** roles of water as a solvent in living organisms.
8. Explain why enzymes that are made of different sequences of amino acids catalyse different reactions.
9. Explain how enzyme activity is affected by temperature.

> **Revision tip**
>
> Notice the difference between questions 6 and 9. For question 6, you just need to state what happens to enzyme activity at different temperatures. For question 9, you need to explain *why* this happens.

1 Animals and plants belong to different kingdoms.

(a) The diagram shows a lobster, which belongs to the animal kingdom. The binomial of this organism is *Homarus americanus*.

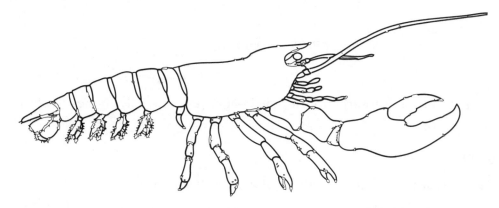

(i) State **one** feature, visible in the diagram, which shows that the organism is:

- an arthropod [1]
- a crustacean [1]

(ii) Name the genus to which this organism belongs. [1]

(b) There are several different species of lobsters.

Explain how a biologist could decide whether two types of lobster belong to the same species, or to different species. [2]

(c) The diagram shows a group of cells.

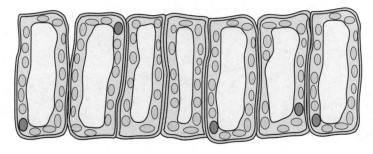

(i) Describe **two** features, visible in the diagram, that show that the organism from which this group of cells was taken belongs to the plant kingdom. [2]

(ii) Give the biological term for a group of similar cells, such as those shown in the diagram. [1]

(iii) Measure the total width of the group of cells in the diagram, in mm.
The magnification of the diagram is ×800.
Calculate the actual width of the group of cells, in mm.
Show your working. [2]

2 **(a) (i)** Define the term *diffusion*. [3]

(ii) List **two** ways in which active transport differs from diffusion. [2]

(b) A Petri dish was filled with agar jelly containing starch. A hole was cut in the centre of the starch–agar jelly. Ten drops of iodine solution were placed in the hole.

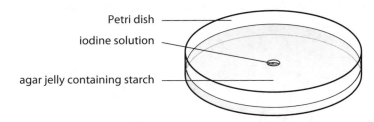

Petri dish

iodine solution

agar jelly containing starch

As the iodine solution diffused into the starch–agar jelly, the jelly changed colour. State the colour of:

(i) the iodine solution. [1]

(ii) the starch–agar jelly after the iodine solution diffused into it. [1]

(c) Outline **one** way in which the diffusion of gases is important to living organisms. [2]

Supplement

3 The diagram shows an animal cell.

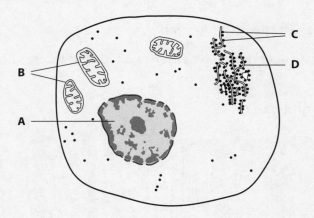

B

A

C

D

(a) Name structures **B** and **D**. [2]

(b) Sperm cells contain more of the structures labelled B than egg cells.
Explain why. [3]

(c) Structure **A** is a nucleus. It contains DNA.

(i) Outline the function of the nucleus in a cell. [1]

(ii) Explain how DNA can be used to help to classify organisms. [2]

(d) The actual length of structure **B** is 9 μm.
Measure the length of structure **B** on the diagram above.
Use your measurement to calculate the magnification of the diagram.
Show your working. [2]

4 (a) Define the term *osmosis*. [3]

(b) Osmosis takes place more quickly at 40 °C than at 10 °C. Explain why. [2]

(c) Explain the importance of water potential and osmosis in the uptake of water by plants. [3]

(d) A plant growing in a pot was not watered for several days. The leaves of the plant wilted (became soft and hung downwards).
Explain why this happened. [4]

5 (a) Describe how you could test a food sample for the presence of fats. [2]

(b) The enzyme lipase converts fats to fatty acids and glycerol.

A student measured 5 cm³ of lipase solution and 1 cm³ of indicator solution into five test tubes. She placed each tube into a water bath at one of five temperatures. She measured 5 cm³ of milk into five more test tubes, and again placed one tube in each of the five water baths.

After 20 minutes, the student poured the milk into the enzyme–indicator mixture that had been kept in the same water bath. She timed how long it took for the indicator to change colour.

The indicator that the student used is pink at a pH above 8, and colourless at a pH below 8.

The table shows the student's results.

Temperature / °C	Time taken to go colourless / min
0	24
20	11
40	3
60	39
80	did not change colour

(i) Suggest why the student kept all the tubes in the water baths for 20 minutes before pouring the milk into the enzyme–indicator mixture. [1]

(ii) The student used a stopwatch calibrated in seconds to time the experiment. Suggest why she recorded the time taken to go colourless to the nearest minute, rather than in seconds. [1]

(iii) Explain why the mixture became colourless in the tube kept at 20 °C. [2]

(iv) Explain why the mixture took longer to become colourless in the tube kept at 20 °C than in the tube kept at 40 °C. [2]

(v) Explain why the mixture did not change colour in the tube kept at 80 °C. [2]

(vi) Suggest what the student could do next, in order to obtain a more precise value for the optimum temperature of this enzyme. [2]

Plant nutrition

Plants make carbohydrates by **photosynthesis**. This requires energy from light, which is absorbed by the green pigment **chlorophyll**. Chlorophyll is found inside chloroplasts inside plant cells.

Definition
Photosynthesis – the process by which plants manufacture carbohydrates from raw materials using energy from light.

The word equation for photosynthesis is:

carbon dioxide + water $\longrightarrow$ glucose + oxygen

Supplement

The balanced chemical equation for photosynthesis is:

$$6CO_2 + 6H_2O \xrightarrow[\text{chlorophyll}]{\text{light}} C_6H_{12}O_6 + 6O_2$$

In photosynthesis, chlorophyll helps to transfer energy from light into chemical energy in carbohydrates.

The glucose made in photosynthesis is used to:

- make starch, by linking many glucose molecules together; starch is stored inside plant cells for later use, for example as an energy source;
- make cellulose, by linking many glucose molecules together in a different way; cellulose is used to make plant cell walls;
- make sucrose, which is used to transport carbohydrates from one part of a plant to another;
- make lipids, by rearranging the carbon, hydrogen and oxygen atoms; lipids can be stored for later use as an energy source;
- make amino acids, by rearranging the carbon, hydrogen and oxygen atoms and adding nitrogen; amino acids are used to make proteins, which are used for building new cells, for active transport and as enzymes.

To determine whether a leaf has been photosynthesising, you can test it for starch.

1 Place the leaf in boiling water. This destroys the waxy cuticle and breaks open the cell membranes.

2 Place the leaf in hot alcohol. This dissolves the chlorophyll from the leaf.

3 Dip the now colourless, brittle leaf into water to soften it.

4 Add iodine solution, and look for a blue-black colour.

Investigating what is needed for photosynthesis

If a variegated (green and white) leaf is tested for starch, only the parts that were green go blue-black. This shows that chlorophyll is needed for photosynthesis.

To investigate the necessity of light for photosynthesis, partly cover a leaf on a plant with black paper and stand the plant in a light place for a day. Then remove the leaf from the plant and test for starch. Only the parts that were uncovered go blue-black.

To investigate the necessity of carbon dioxide for photosynthesis, you can use a substance that absorbs carbon dioxide (such as soda lime) to remove all the carbon dioxide from the air. Place one plant in a container with soda lime, and another plant in an identical container with no soda lime. Test a leaf from both plants for starch. Only the leaf that had carbon dioxide goes blue-black.

In each of these experiments, a **control** is used. A control is something with which we can compare the results. For example, in the black paper experiment, we can compare the results for the parts of the leaf that had light with the parts that did not have light.

Investigating the effects of variables on the rate of photosynthesis

Aquatic plants (ones that live in water) are useful for investigating the rate of photosynthesis. The oxygen that they make in photosynthesis is given off as bubbles. You can count how many bubbles are produced in a set amount of time, or collect the oxygen in a gas syringe and measure the volume produced in a set amount of time.

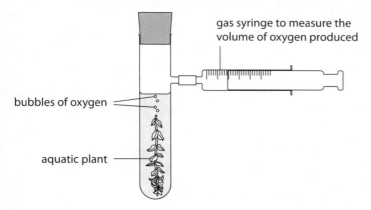

The effect of light intensity can be investigated by using a lamp placed at different measured distances from the plant. The closer the lamp, the greater the light intensity.

The effect of temperature can be investigated by changing the temperature of the water surrounding the plant.

The effect of carbon dioxide concentration can be investigated by adding different quantities of sodium hydrogencarbonate to the water surrounding the plant. This decomposes in water to give off carbon dioxide.

Revision tip

For the light and carbon dioxide experiments, it is best to start off with a plant that does not contain any starch, so that you can be sure that any starch you find has been made during your experiment. To do this, keep the plant in the dark for a few days before you do your experiment.

Revision tip

In all of these experiments, it is important to make sure that only the variable you are investigating is changed. For example, when investigating *light intensity*, keep the *temperature* of the water around the plant the same by standing the test tube inside a water bath.

1 How light intensity affects rate of photosynthesis

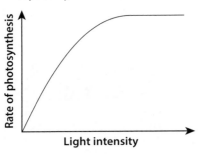

2 How temperature affects rate of photosynthesis

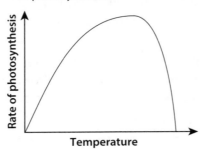

3 How carbon dioxide concentration affects rate of photosynthesis

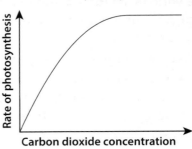

Limiting factors

The rate at which a plant can photosynthesise is determined by the factor that is in the shortest supply. For example, a plant may have plenty of light, but cannot use it all because it does not have enough carbon dioxide.

> **Definition**
>
> **Limiting factor** – something present in the environment in such short supply that it restricts life processes.

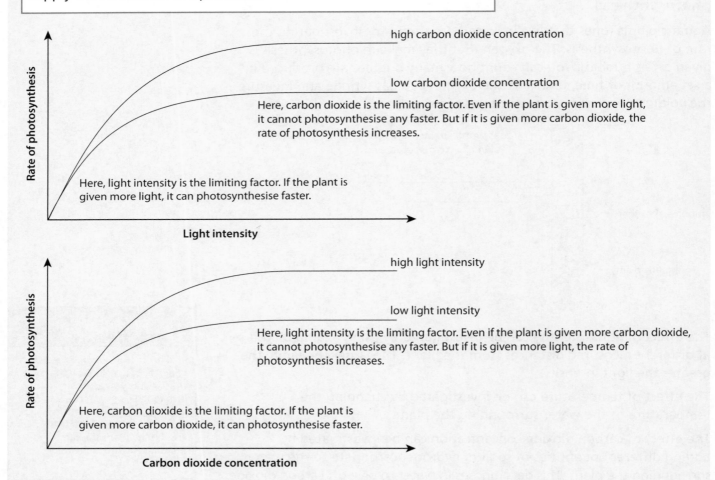

High-value crops are often grown in glasshouses. This allows the conditions to be controlled, to maximise the rate of photosynthesis. The faster photosynthesis takes place, the faster the plants can grow, so yields increase.

For example, in a temperate country, light intensity or low temperature may be limiting factors in winter. In a glasshouse, more light and higher temperatures can be provided.

In a tropical country, carbon dioxide concentration or high temperature may be limiting factors. In a glasshouse, more carbon dioxide and lower temperatures can be provided.

Respiration and photosynthesis

Like all living organisms, plants respire. They take in oxygen and give out carbon dioxide.

However, in daylight, the rate of photosynthesis is greater than the rate of respiration. This means that:

- All of the carbon dioxide that is produced by respiration is used in photosynthesis, and the plant also takes in more carbon dioxide from its surroundings.
- Some of the oxygen released by photosynthesis is used up in respiration, but not all of it; the rest of the oxygen is given off from the plant.

In darkness, only respiration takes place.

The uptake and loss of carbon dioxide and oxygen is called **gas exchange**.

> ### Revision tip
> Remember that plants, like all living organisms, respire all the time. But they only photosynthesise when they have light.

You can use **hydrogencarbonate indicator** to investigate the effect of gas exchange in an aquatic plant. This indicator is yellow when there is a lot of carbon dioxide, and red or purple when there is little or no carbon dioxide.

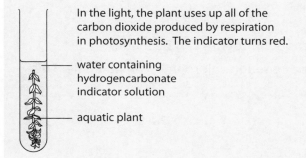

In the light, the plant uses up all of the carbon dioxide produced by respiration in photosynthesis. The indicator turns red.

— water containing hydrogencarbonate indicator solution

— aquatic plant

In the dark, carbon dioxide is given off in respiration and not used in photosynthesis. The indicator turns yellow.

— black paper covering tube with aquatic plant and water containing hydrogencarbonate indicator solution

Leaves

The diagram shows the structure of a leaf of a dicotyledonous plant.

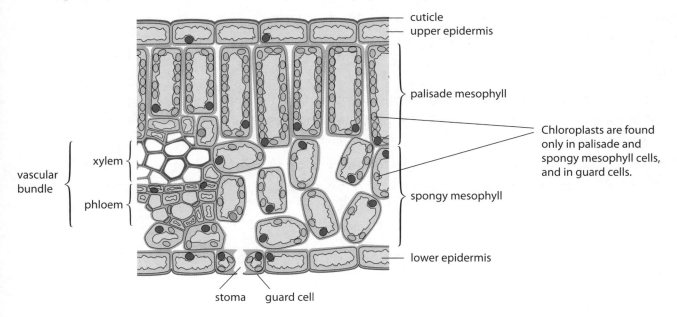

cuticle
upper epidermis
palisade mesophyll
Chloroplasts are found only in palisade and spongy mesophyll cells, and in guard cells.
vascular bundle
xylem
phloem
spongy mesophyll
lower epidermis
stoma   guard cell

The **upper epidermis** does not have chloroplasts, so light passes through to the palisade cells. The upper epidermis secretes a waxy cuticle, which prevents water loss from the leaf surface.

Most photosynthesis takes place inside **palisade cells**. These:

- are near the top of the leaf, so get plenty of sunlight
- have many chloroplasts, which absorb energy from sunlight
- have air spaces close to them, to provide carbon dioxide.

Some photosynthesis takes place inside **spongy mesophyll cells**. These have large **air spaces** between them, to allow carbon dioxide to diffuse to the palisade cells from the stomata.

Water is provided by the **xylem** tissue. Sucrose, made in photosynthesis, is transported away in the **phloem** tissue.

Carbon dioxide enters by diffusion through the **stomata** (singular: stoma). The **guard cells** can change shape to open or close the stomata.

Mineral requirements

Plants obtain mineral ions from the soil.

Nitrate ions are needed for making amino acids, which can then be used to make proteins.

Magnesium ions are used for making chlorophyll.

Nitrate ion deficiency results in weak growth, because not enough proteins can be made.

Magnesium ion deficiency results in yellow leaves, because not enough chlorophyll can be made. This means that there is less photosynthesis, so growth is weak.

Quick test

1. Write the word equation for photosynthesis.
2. Why is an aquatic plant used, when investigating the effect of light intensity on the rate of photosynthesis?
3. Describe how temperature affects the rate of photosynthesis.
4. Name **three** tissues in a leaf where the cells contain chloroplasts.
5. Why do plants need magnesium ions?

Supplement

6. Write the balanced chemical equation for photosynthesis.
7. In what form do plants (a) store and (b) transport carbohydrates?
8. What is a *limiting factor*?
9. List three things that can be limiting factors for photosynthesis.
10. Explain how air spaces help to adapt a leaf for photosynthesis.

Human diet and digestion

A **balanced diet** is one that contains some of all the different nutrients, in suitable proportions, and with a suitable quantity of energy. The table shows information about these nutrients.

Nutrient	Examples of good sources	Function	Notes
carbohydrate	bread, rice, potatoes, pasta	energy release in respiration	
fats	plant oils, fatty meat	energy storage; making cell membranes	high levels of saturated fat in the diet may increase the risk of coronary heart disease
proteins	meat, fish, pulses, dairy products, eggs	building cells, making enzymes, making haemoglobin; can also provide energy	
vitamin C	citrus fruits	making collagen (an elastic protein found in skin and bones)	lack of vitamin C causes scurvy
vitamin D	dairy products; formed in skin when sunlight falls onto it	helps calcium to be absorbed, so important for strong bones	lack of vitamin D causes rickets
calcium	dairy products	strong bones and teeth	
iron	red meat, dark green vegetables	making haemoglobin	lack of iron causes anaemia
fibre (roughage)	fruit, vegetables, brown rice	helps the muscles in the alimentary canal to work	lack of fibre causes constipation
water	drinks, most foods	as a solvent	

The dietary needs of a person are affected by:

- age: younger people need more protein for growth; older people may need less energy intake if they become less active;
- gender: in general, men tend to need more energy intake than women;
- pregnancy and breast-feeding: during pregnancy, a woman needs plenty of protein, vitamins and minerals to supply her fetus and young baby; she also needs a little extra energy intake;
- activity: the more active a person's lifestyle, the more energy intake they require in their diet.

Too great an energy intake can result in a person becoming obese. This increases the risk of developing various illnesses, including diabetes and coronary heart disease.

Too low an energy and protein intake can result in starvation, when the body breaks down muscles and other structures in order to keep cells alive.

> ### Revision tip
>
> Try to use the word 'nutrient' when you are referring to one of the nine nutrients listed in the table. The word 'food' should be used for things that you eat, such as rice. Food contains nutrients.

Supplement

A very low protein intake can result in **kwashiorkor**. The person has a very low body weight but may have a swollen abdomen. A very low energy intake can result in **marasmus**. The person has a very low body weight and looks emaciated.

The digestive system

The diagram shows the structure of the digestive system. The annotations summarise what happens in each part.

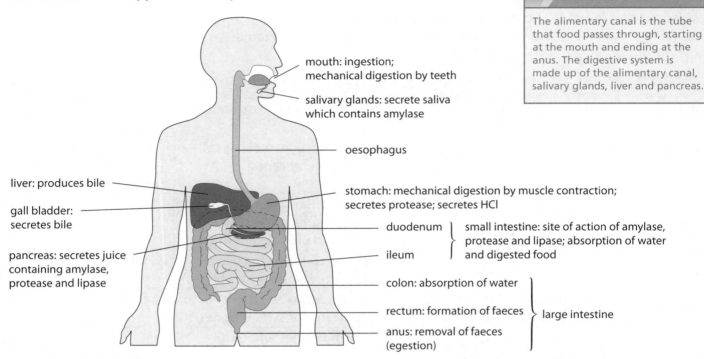

mouth: ingestion; mechanical digestion by teeth

salivary glands: secrete saliva which contains amylase

oesophagus

liver: produces bile

gall bladder: secretes bile

pancreas: secretes juice containing amylase, protease and lipase

stomach: mechanical digestion by muscle contraction; secretes protease; secretes HCl

duodenum

ileum

small intestine: site of action of amylase, protease and lipase; absorption of water and digested food

colon: absorption of water

rectum: formation of faeces

anus: removal of faeces (egestion)

large intestine

> ### Revision tip
>
> The alimentary canal is the tube that food passes through, starting at the mouth and ending at the anus. The digestive system is made up of the alimentary canal, salivary glands, liver and pancreas.

Definitions

Ingestion – taking substances, for example food and drink, into the body through the mouth.

Mechanical digestion – breakdown of food into smaller pieces without chemical change to the food molecules.

Chemical digestion – breakdown of large, insoluble molecules into small, soluble molecules.

Absorption – movement of small food molecules and ions through the wall of the intestine into the blood.

Assimilation – movement of digested food molecules into the cells of the body where they are used, becoming part of the cells.

Egestion – passing out of food that has not been digested or absorbed, as faeces, through the anus.

Teeth

Humans have four types of teeth. Teeth help with ingestion and mechanical digestion.

Incisors are at the front of the mouth. They are chisel-shaped and bite off pieces of food.

Canines are just behind the incisors. They are more pointed and help to bite and hold food.

Premolars and molars are at the sides and back of the mouth. They have broad, ridged surfaces that grind food into smaller pieces.

Dental decay happens when acid dissolves the enamel and dentine. This can happen if food remains (particularly sugary foods) are left on or between the teeth. Bacteria on the teeth break down sugars by respiration, producing acid.

enamel: hardest substance in the body; can be dissolved by acids

dentine: similar to bone; contains living cells

gums

pulp cavity: contains nerves and blood vessels, to supply the living cells in the dentine with nutrients and oxygen

cement: contains fibres that attach the tooth to the jawbone

This can be avoided by:

- not eating too many sugary foods
- brushing teeth regularly to remove food remains.

Chemical digestion

Polysaccharides, proteins and fats are made up of large molecules. These must be broken down to smaller molecules before they can be absorbed. This is chemical digestion, and it is done by enzymes.

Amylase breaks down starch to simple sugars.

Protease breaks down proteins to amino acids.

Lipase breaks down fats to fatty acids and glycerol.

See the diagram on page 30 to remind yourself where these enzymes are secreted and where they work.

The protease in the stomach has a low optimum pH. This is provided by the secretion of hydrochloric acid, which also kills bacteria present in the food by denaturing their enzymes.

Supplement

In carbohydrate digestion:

- **amylase** breaks down starch to the disaccharide maltose;
- **maltase** breaks down maltose to the monosaccharide glucose.

Amylase is secreted from the salivary glands into the mouth, and is also secreted from the pancreas into pancreatic juice, which flows into the small intestine.

Maltase is secreted by the epithelial cells covering the villi in the small intestine.

> **Revision tip**
>
> Note that amylase usually produces maltose, not glucose, when it digests starch. However, some forms of amylase made by bacteria or fungi do produce some glucose.

In protein digestion:

- **pepsin** is a protease secreted in the stomach; it has a low optimum pH which is provided by the secretion of HCl;
- **trypsin** is a protease secreted by the pancreas into pancreatic juice; it works in the small intestine.

Bile is a liquid secreted by the liver and stored in the gall bladder. It flows along the bile duct into the duodenum.

Bile contains:

- **sodium hydrogencarbonate**, which is a base and neutralises the acidic mixture of food and gastric juice entering the duodenum from the stomach; this provides a suitable pH for the action of amylase, trypsin and lipase;
- **bile salts**, which break large globules of water-insoluble fats into smaller droplets; these mix with the watery fluids inside the small intestine to produce an emulsion. This increases the surface area of the fat droplets, which enables lipase to access the fat molecules and digest them.

> **Revision tip**
>
> Bile does not contain any enzymes.

Absorption

Absorption of small nutrient molecules and ions – water, vitamins, mineral ions, glucose, amino acids, fatty acids and glycerol – takes place in the small intestine. A relatively small quantity of water is also absorbed in the colon.

During absorption, these small molecules and ions pass through the wall of the small intestine and into the blood.

The lining of the small intestine is covered by tiny folds called villi.

The cells in the epithelium of a villus have tiny folds on them called **microvilli**. Villi and their microvilli greatly increase the surface area of the lining of the small intestine, which increases the rate at which absorption can take place.

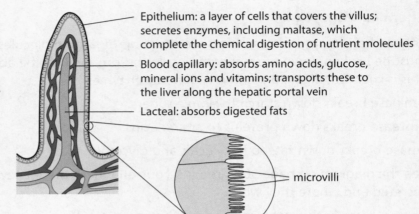

Epithelium: a layer of cells that covers the villus; secretes enzymes, including maltase, which complete the chemical digestion of nutrient molecules

Blood capillary: absorbs amino acids, glucose, mineral ions and vitamins; transports these to the liver along the hepatic portal vein

Lacteal: absorbs digested fats

microvilli

Cholera

Cholera is a disease caused by a bacterium. It causes the loss of watery faeces. This is called diarrhoea. Cholera is a serious disease that can be fatal. It can be treated by using oral rehydration therapy, in which the patient is given drinks containing glucose and salt dissolved in water.

The cholera bacterium produces a toxin (poisonous substance) that causes the cells covering the villi to secrete chloride ions into the small intestine. This decreases the water potential inside the small intestine, so water moves into it from the cells by osmosis, down a water potential gradient. This is why the patient suffers from diarrhoea.

Cholera is dangerous because:

- the patient loses salts from the blood;
- the patient loses a lot of water and becomes severely dehydrated.

Quick test

1. List the **three** classes of nutrient that can provide energy.
2. Name **two** diseases for which there is an increased risk in an obese person.
3. Explain why proteins, fats and carbohydrates need to be digested, but water does not.
4. Name **two** parts of the digestive system that secrete amylase.
5. Name **two** parts of the alimentary canal where amylase digests starch.
6. Name the substance that is produced when amylase digests starch.
7. Name the part of the alimentary canal where most absorption of water takes place.

8. What is kwashiorkor?
9. Name the protease enzyme that has an optimum pH of 2, and state where this protease enzyme is found.
10. Outline **two** functions of bile.
11. Explain how and why the internal surface area of the small intestine is increased.

1 The diagram shows the apparatus used by a student to investigate the effect of carbon dioxide concentration on the rate of photosynthesis of an aquatic plant.

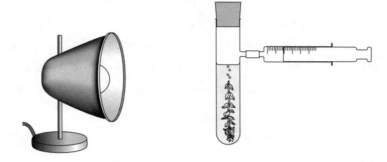

The student used sodium hydrogencarbonate solution to supply the plant with extra carbon dioxide. The student measured the volume of oxygen given off by the plant in five minutes. He then poured out the water from the test tube, and replaced it with 0.2% sodium hydrogencarbonate solution. He repeated this with four other concentrations of sodium hydrogencarbonate solution.
His results are shown in the table.

Concentration of sodium hydrogencarbonate solution (%)	Volume of gas given off in five minutes / cm³	Rate of oxygen production / cm³ per minute
0	2.4	0.48
0.2	3.8	0.76
0.4	5.1	1.02
0.6	6.7	1.34
0.8	7.4	1.48
1.0	7.3	

(a) Complete the table by calculating the rate of oxygen production when 1.0% sodium hydrogencarbonate solution was used. [1]

(b) State the independent variable in the student's experiment. [1]

(c) State **two** variables that the student should have kept constant in his experiment. [2]

(d) Suggest why some oxygen was produced even when the concentration of sodium hydrogencarbonate was zero. [1]

(e) Photosynthesis requires a source of energy to convert raw materials to products. One of these products is oxygen.

Name:

(i) the source of energy in photosynthesis; [1]

(ii) the two raw materials; [2]

(iii) the product, other than oxygen. [1]

2 **(a)** Write the balanced equation for photosynthesis. [2]

(b) Explain the role of chlorophyll in photosynthesis. [2]

(c) An experiment was carried out to find how light intensity affected the mass of tomato fruits produced by plants grown in a glasshouse in a temperate country.
A large number of tomato plants were grown in the same glasshouse. Half of the glasshouse was shaded, so that half the plants were in the shade and half the plants received full sunlight.
After the plants had begun to flower, the dry mass of all the developing fruits on a sample of plants from each area was determined every 10 days. (Dry mass is the mass of the fruits after all water has been removed.)
The results are shown on the graph.

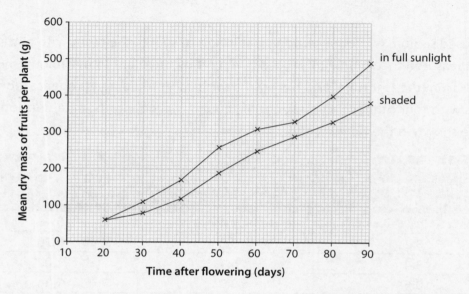

(i) Describe the change in dry mass of the tomato fruits in the shaded area during the experiment.
You will gain credit if you refer to data from the graph in your answer. [3]

(ii) Explain why the dry mass of the fruits was greater in the plants receiving full sunlight. [3]

(iii) Suggest why the results may not have been the same if the experiment was carried out in a tropical country. [2]

(iv) List **three** ways in which the carbohydrates made in photosynthesis would be used to produce the tomato fruits. [3]

3 **(a) (i)** Explain the difference between mechanical digestion and chemical digestion. [2]

(ii) Name **two** parts of the alimentary canal where mechanical digestion takes place. [2]

(b) The stomach secretes protease and hydrochloric acid.

(i) Describe the function of protease in the stomach. [2]

(ii) State the function of hydrochloric acid in the stomach. [2]

(c) The diagram shows part of some cells on the surface of a villus.

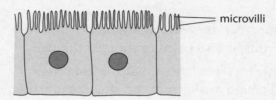

microvilli

(i) Name the part of the alimentary canal where villi are found. [1]

(ii) The cell surface membranes of the cells covering the villi secrete maltase. Describe the function of maltase. [2]

(iii) In mice, a gene affects the length of the microvilli in the alimentary canal. The bar chart shows the mean length of the microvilli in mice with two different alleles (versions) of this gene.

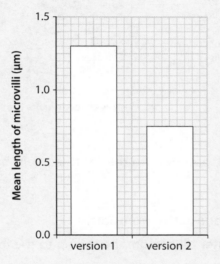

Young mice with version 1 of the gene grew faster than those with version 2 of the gene. Suggest an explanation for this. [4]

Transport in plants

Plants have two transport systems.

Xylem (pronounced zi-lem) transports water and mineral salts from the roots to the leaves, flowers and fruits. It also helps to support the plant.

Phloem (pronounced flo-em) transports substances that the plant has made, in the form of sucrose and amino acids, from the leaves and storage organs to all other parts of the plant.

The diagrams show the positions of xylem in cross-sections of a stem and a root. The diagram on page 27 shows the positions of xylem and phloem in a leaf.

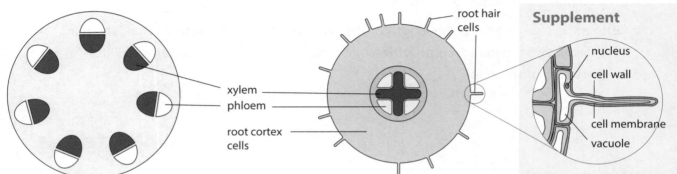

Cross-section of a stem   Cross-section of a root

Supplement

The root hair cells are very small, and there are thousands of them. This increases their surface area, which increases the rate at which water is absorbed by osmosis, through their partially permeable cell membranes.

These membranes also move mineral ions – such as nitrate ions and magnesium ions – into the root hair cell by active transport.

Water uptake

Water enters the plant from the soil, passing into the root hair cells by osmosis. Root hair cells:

- absorb water by osmosis;
- absorb mineral ions by diffusion and active transport.

The diagram shows the path that water takes from the soil up to the leaves.

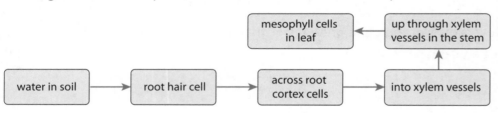

You can see this happening if you stand a celery stalk in coloured water. As the water moves up the stalk, you can see the colour moving upwards through the stem and into the veins in the leaves. If you cut the stalk across, you can see little coloured dots. These are the xylem vessels through which the coloured water is flowing upwards.

Transpiration

When the water reaches the leaves, a very small amount of it is used in photosynthesis. Most of the water moves out of the leaves into the air, in the form of water vapour. This is called **transpiration**.

Transpiration – the loss of water vapour from plant leaves by evaporation of water at the surfaces of the mesophyll cells followed by diffusion of water vapour through the stomata.

In the leaf:

- Water moves out of the xylem vessels and into the palisade mesophyll and spongy mesophyll cells by osmosis.
- Water seeps into the cell walls of the mesophyll cells.
- Some of the water in these cell walls evaporates (changes from liquid water to water vapour).
- This produces a very high humidity in the air spaces in the leaf (that is, there is a lot of water vapour in these air spaces).
- The water vapour diffuses out of the air spaces, through the stomata, into the air.

Revision tip

Remember that water diffuses out of the leaf as water vapour, not liquid water.

Supplement

Significance of large surface area of mesophyll cells

The large surface area of the mesophyll cells inside the leaf means that a lot of water can evaporate in a short period of time. The interconnecting air spaces inside the leaf mean that the water vapour can easily diffuse through the leaf and out into the air through the stomata.

Transpiration pull and cohesion

Transpiration provides the pulling force that makes water flow up through the xylem vessels. When water vapour diffuses out through the stomata, it decreases the water potential inside the leaf. Because there is less water in the leaf, the water pressure at the top of the xylem is reduced, so that it is less than the pressure at the base of the xylem vessel, in the root. Water therefore flows from the bottom of the xylem vessels (high pressure) to the top of the xylem vessels (low pressure). We call the force that produces this flow **transpiration pull**.

The water flows up in an unbroken column. It can do this because water molecules are attracted to each other and held together by **cohesion**.

Revision tip

Transpiration pull is similar to the 'pull' you exert when you suck a drink up a straw. Sucking at the top of the straw reduces the pressure, so the drink flows up the straw from relatively high pressure at the bottom to lower pressure at the top.

Wilting

Leaves are normally held out flat, to expose the maximum area to sunlight, for photosynthesis. They are supported by:

- turgor pressure in the mesophyll cells;
- xylem vessels in the veins of the leaf.

If transpiration happens faster than water can be drawn up from the soil, the leaf cells don't have enough water and become flaccid. The leaf loses its firm structure, and becomes soft and floppy. The plant **wilts**.

Wilting can help a plant to survive when it is short of water. When the leaves collapse, they expose less surface area to the air. This decreases the rate at which transpiration occurs, so the plant loses less water.

Investigating transpiration rate

The diagrams show two ways of measuring how quickly a plant loses water by transpiration.

As a plant loses water, it loses weight. We can record the weight loss over a period of time, which tells us the mass of water vapour that has gone out of the leaves by transpiration. The surface of the soil must be covered so that no water is lost from there, only from the plant.

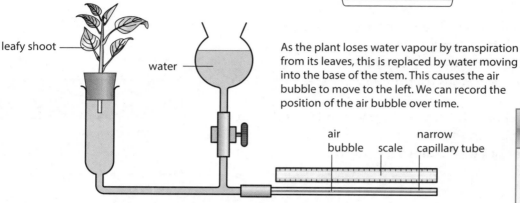

As the plant loses water vapour by transpiration from its leaves, this is replaced by water moving into the base of the stem. This causes the air bubble to move to the left. We can record the position of the air bubble over time.

Potometer – apparatus for measuring the rate of water uptake by a shoot

The rate of transpiration is affected by:

- **temperature**: high temperature speeds up transpiration;
- **humidity**: high humidity slows down transpiration.

Supplement

High temperatures speed up the rate of transpiration because water molecules have more kinetic energy at high temperatures. This speeds up evaporation on the surfaces of the mesophyll cells, and also speeds up the diffusion of water vapour through the leaf and out through the stomata.

High humidity slows down the rate of transpiration because it decreases the water potential gradient from the leaf to the air. The air spaces inside the leaf always have a high humidity – that is, there are always a lot of water molecules in the air inside the leaf, so it has a high water potential. High humidity means that there are a lot of water molecules in the air outside the leaf, so it has a relatively high water potential. So the higher the humidity, the less the difference in water potential between the air inside and outside the leaf. This decreases the rate of diffusion of the water molecules.

Translocation

Translocation is the transport of substances that the plant has made. These include:

- **sucrose** – photosynthesis produces the monosaccharide glucose. This is converted to the disaccharide sucrose, which moves into the phloem to be transported to all other parts of the plant;
- **amino acids** – these are made by combining glucose with nitrate ions.

> **Definition**
>
> **Translocation** – the movement of sucrose and amino acids in phloem:
> - from regions of production (source)
> - to regions of storage or to regions where they are used in respiration or growth (sink).

Sources and sinks

A **source** is a part of a plant from which sucrose or amino acids are being transported.

A **sink** is a part of a plant to which sucrose or amino acids are being transported.

Sources and sinks can be in different places at different times of year.

When a plant is photosynthesising, for example in summer in a temperate country, a lot of sucrose is produced in the leaves. The leaves are a source.

The sucrose could be transported to:

* the roots, where it is changed into starch and stored;
* flowers or fruits, where it is changed into fructose for nectar or to make the fruits sweet;
* any part of the plant that requires energy; the sucrose is converted to glucose and used in respiration to release energy.

The roots, flowers, or fruits are sinks.

When a plant is not photosynthesising, for example in winter in a temperate country, the main source is the areas where starch has been stored, for example the roots.

The starch is broken down to produce sucrose, which is then transported to the leaves. The sucrose is converted to glucose and used in respiration to release energy.

The leaves are a sink.

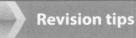

Revision tips

Remember:
* glucose is the carbohydrate that is made by photosynthesis, and can be used in respiration to release energy;
* sucrose is the form in which carbohydrates are transported around a plant;
* starch is the carbohydrate that is used as an energy store.

Quick test

1. Xylem is one of the two transport systems of a plant. Name the other.
2. State **two** functions of xylem.
3. Sketch a diagram of a cross-section of a stem, and label the positions of xylem and phloem.
4. Put these parts of the plant in order, to describe the pathway taken by water as it travels from the soil to the air outside the plant:
   leaf mesophyll cells, xylem, root hair cells, root cortex cells
5. Define *transpiration*.

6. Name the processes by which root hair cells absorb:
   (a) water;
   (b) mineral ions.
7. Explain how transpiration helps water to move up through xylem.
8. Explain how cohesion helps water to move up through xylem.
9. Explain why high temperature speeds up the rate of transpiration.
10. Explain why a plant's roots can be a source at one time of year, and a sink at another time of year.

Transport in animals

In mammals, the circulatory system is made up of:

- a series of tubes, called **blood vessels**, through which blood flows;
- the **heart**, which is a pump that moves the blood through the blood vessels;
- **valves**, which make sure that blood always moves in the same direction.

Supplement
Single and double circulations

The diagrams show the circulatory systems of a fish and a mammal.

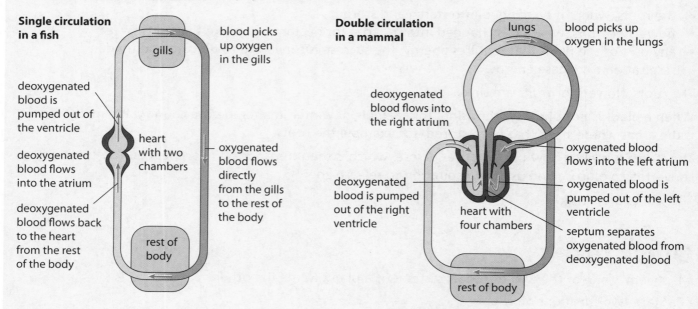

Single circulation in a fish

- deoxygenated blood is pumped out of the ventricle
- deoxygenated blood flows into the atrium
- deoxygenated blood flows back to the heart from the rest of the body

gills

heart with two chambers

rest of body

blood picks up oxygen in the gills

oxygenated blood flows directly from the gills to the rest of the body

Double circulation in a mammal

- deoxygenated blood flows into the right atrium
- deoxygenated blood is pumped out of the right ventricle

lungs

heart with four chambers

rest of body

blood picks up oxygen in the lungs

oxygenated blood flows into the left atrium

oxygenated blood is pumped out of the left ventricle

septum separates oxygenated blood from deoxygenated blood

In a **single circulation**, the blood passes through the heart once on a complete journey around the body.

In a **double circulation**, the blood passes through the heart twice on a complete journey around the body.

In a double circulation, the blood goes back to the heart after being oxygenated. This is more efficient at getting oxygen to the body cells, because the oxygenated blood is given an extra 'push' to move it quickly to these cells.

The heart

The diagram shows a section through a heart, looking from the front of a person's body.

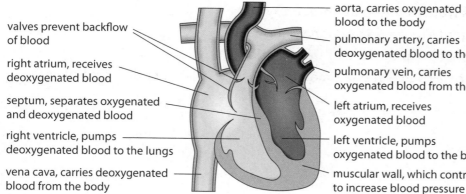

- valves prevent backflow of blood
- right atrium, receives deoxygenated blood
- septum, separates oxygenated and deoxygenated blood
- right ventricle, pumps deoxygenated blood to the lungs
- vena cava, carries deoxygenated blood from the body

- aorta, carries oxygenated blood to the body
- pulmonary artery, carries deoxygenated blood to the lungs
- pulmonary vein, carries oxygenated blood from the lungs
- left atrium, receives oxygenated blood
- left ventricle, pumps oxygenated blood to the body
- muscular wall, which contracts to increase blood pressure

Supplement

The valves in the entrances to the aorta and pulmonary artery are called **semilunar valves**.

The valves between the atria and ventricles are called **atrioventricular valves**.

The walls of the heart are made of muscle. When the muscle contracts, the walls of the heart squeeze the blood and push it out.

The blood moves out of the heart into arteries, which carry blood away from the heart. Blood flows back to the heart in veins.

We can monitor the activity of the heart by:

- recording the electrical activity of the heart as an ECG;
- measuring the pulse rate;
- listening to the sounds of the valves closing.

Supplement

The muscular walls of the ventricles are much thicker than those of the atria. This is because the atria only have to produce enough force to push the blood into the ventricles. The ventricles have to produce enough force to push the blood out of the heart and then to the lungs or the rest of the body.

The muscular wall of the left ventricle is thicker than that of the right ventricle. This is because the left ventricle has to produce enough force to give the blood sufficient pressure to pass all around the body. The right ventricle only pushes the blood to the lungs, so not as much pressure is needed.

This is what happens during one heart beat.

1. The blood flows into the left atrium and the right atrium from the pulmonary vein and the vena cava.

2. The muscles in the walls of both the atria contract, forcing the blood down into the ventricles. The pressure of the blood forces the atrioventricular valves open, allowing it to flow through.

3. The muscles in the walls of both ventricles contract, forcing the blood up into the aorta and the pulmonary artery. The pressure of the blood forces the semilunar valves open, allowing it to flow through. The pressure of the blood also pushes up onto the atrioventricular valves, which snap shut, so the blood cannot go back up into the atria.

Revision tips

- The valves can only open in one direction, like doors that only swing one way. When they are pushed in that direction, they swing open. When they are pushed the other way, they swing shut.
- The valves don't open and close themselves. They are pushed open or closed by the pressure of the blood.

Effect of physical activity on heart rate

When you exercise, your heart beats faster. You can measure this by measuring the pulse rate. You can measure your pulse by touching one of the arteries in your neck. Count how many pulses you can feel in 30 seconds, and multiply by two.

The graph shows what happens to your heart rate when you exercise.

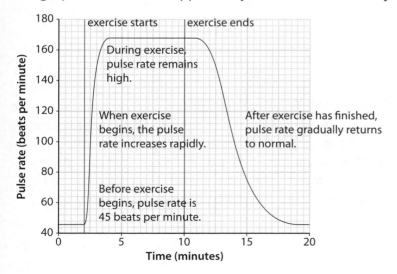

The graph below explains why the pulse rate changes when you exercise.

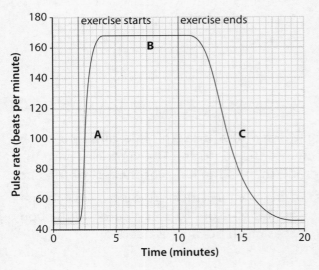

A When you start to exercise, muscles in your legs contract. They need extra energy for this, so they must respire faster to release this energy. This will be aerobic respiration, so they need extra oxygen, so the heart beats faster to deliver more oxygen to them. They produce a lot of carbon dioxide, and the faster heart rate helps to remove this and take it to the lungs to be excreted.

B The muscles continue to respire rapidly throughout the exercise period, so the pulse rate remains high. The muscle cells will release energy by aerobic respiration, as long as they have enough oxygen. But if not enough oxygen reaches them, they will also use anaerobic respiration. This produces lactic acid.

C When exercise stops, the muscles slow down their rate of respiration. But the lactic acid that has built up must now be broken down. This is done by using oxygen, so the pulse rate remains high to deliver this extra oxygen. This is called an oxygen debt. The pulse rate only returns to normal after all the lactic acid has been broken down.

Coronary heart disease

The coronary arteries can be seen on the outside of the heart. They carry oxygenated blood to the heart muscle. This enables the heart muscle cells to release energy by respiration, using oxygen. The muscle cells need energy to be able to contract.

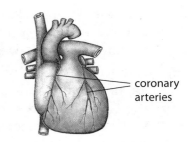

coronary arteries

The coronary arteries can become blocked by blood clots or plaques. The plaques contain cholesterol. If this happens, the heart muscle does not get enough oxygen, so it cannot respire and has no energy to contract. This is called **coronary heart disease** (CHD).

The risk of developing CHD is increased by:

- eating a diet that contains a lot of saturated fat or cholesterol, particularly if too much food is eaten and the person becomes overweight
- not doing enough exercise
- smoking
- having too much stress
- getting older
- being male rather than female
- having genes that make you more likely to get CHD.

Evidence for CHD risk factors
The evidence for the roles of diet and exercise as risk factors for CHD is mixed.

It is impossible to do controlled experiments in which only diet is varied. For example, people also vary in their genetic make-up, and we cannot control that. The best we can do is to collect information about the diets that people eat, and then look for correlations between diet and heart disease. Many studies that have been done indicate that diets rich in saturated fats and cholesterol increase the risk of CHD, but there are some studies that do not support this view. Scientists continue to work on this problem.

The evidence that doing plenty of exercise decreases the risk of CHD is stronger, and most researchers would agree that all the data point to regular exercise reducing the risk of CHD.

Treating CHD

There are several possible treatments for a person who has CHD.

- They can be given drugs, such as **aspirin**, that reduce the likelihood of a blood clot forming and blocking a coronary artery.
- They can be given surgery to remove the blockage and open up the coronary artery. This is called **angioplasty**. A little tube called a **stent** may be inserted, which holds the blood vessel open.
- They can be given surgery to add an extra blood vessel that **bypasses** the blockage. The blood vessel is often a vein taken from the leg.

Blood and lymphatic vessels

The diagram shows the major blood vessels in the human body.

Blood flows out of the heart through arteries, then into tiny capillaries, which deliver the blood close to every cell in the body. The blood then flows into veins, which return it to the heart.

Arteries have thick, muscular walls and relatively narrow **lumen** (the space in the middle through which blood flows).

Veins have much thinner walls. They also have valves.

Capillaries are tiny compared with arteries and veins. Their walls are only one cell thick.

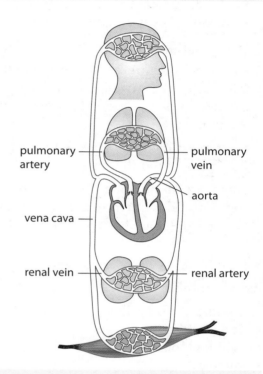

pulmonary artery — pulmonary vein

aorta

vena cava —

renal vein — renal artery

Supplement

Arteries carry blood at high pressure that fluctuates – that is, the pressure increases and decreases as the heart muscle contracts and relaxes. Arteries therefore need:

- thick walls to withstand the high pressure of the blood;
- elastic tissue in their walls, which can expand and recoil as the blood pulses through;
- a narrow lumen, so that the high-pressure blood speeds quickly to the body tissues or lungs.

Arteries divide to form smaller vessels, called **arterioles**. These have the same structure as arteries, but are smaller. They have smooth muscle tissue in their walls. This can contract, closing off the blood vessel, so that blood is diverted to a different area. **Shunt vessels** are arterioles that act as an alternative route for the blood when an arteriole is closed.

> **Revision tip**
>
> The recoil of the elastic tissue in artery walls helps to keep the blood pressure high between pulses, so it evens out the flow of the blood.

> **Revision tip**
>
> The muscle in the walls of blood vessels does **not** help to pump blood.

Arterioles divide to form tiny capillaries. Capillaries have:

- walls that are only one cell thick, and have small gaps in them, so that materials such as oxygen, carbon dioxide and soluble nutrients can easily move through them to pass to or from the body cells;
- a narrow lumen, so that the vessels can penetrate deep into the tissues and get close to every cell; and also so that red blood cells inside the lumen are always close to the walls, so they can give up their oxygen quickly.

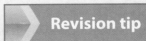

Revision tip

Don't say that capillaries are only one cell thick. It is their walls that are only one cell thick.

Capillaries join up to form **venules,** and these join to form veins. By this time, the blood has lost most of its pressure. Veins therefore do not need thick walls. They do need:

- a wide lumen, to provide as little resistance as possible to the blood flowing through them;
- valves, to keep the blood flowing in the right direction.

The lymphatic system

Blood leaks out of capillaries, filling the spaces between the body cells and forming **tissue fluid**. This is important in providing a suitable environment for the body cells, and allowing substances such as oxygen, carbon dioxide, glucose and urea to diffuse from the blood to the cells, and from the cells to the blood.

The tissue fluid is collected into small, blind-ending vessels called **lymphatic vessels**. These carry tissue fluid back to the thorax (chest), where it is emptied back into the blood system.

There are **lymph nodes** in various places along these lymphatic vessels. They contain high concentrations of white blood cells, which are important in the immune response (see below), which protects the body from infection.

Blood

Blood contains:

- **plasma**, a pale yellow fluid in which the blood cells float
- **red blood cells**
- **white blood cells**
- **platelets.**

Red blood cells

These are small cells with no nucleus. They contain a red pigment called haemoglobin. Haemoglobin combines with oxygen in the lungs, and releases it in the body tissues. This ensures that body cells receive oxygen for respiration.

The lack of a nucleus makes more space for haemoglobin. The cells are shaped like a biconcave disc, which increases their surface area and speeds up the diffusion of oxygen into and out of the red blood cell.

red blood cell

White blood cells

These are usually larger than red blood cells, and they always have a nucleus. White blood cells help to protect the body against disease by:

- Engulfing and digesting pathogens (disease-causing organisms); this is called **phagocytosis**.

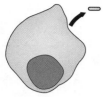

1 A phagocyte moves towards a bacterium

2 The phagocyte pushes a sleeve of cytoplasm outwards to surround the bacterium

3 The bacterium is now enclosed in a vacuole inside the cell. It is then killed and digested by enzymes

- Producing **antibodies**, which attach to pathogens and help to destroy them.

Platelets

These are tiny cell fragments that help the blood to clot.

Supplement

Blood clots when a blood vessel is cut. Blood clotting helps to prevent blood loss, and prevent the entry of pathogens.

When blood clots, a soluble protein in the blood plasma, called **fibrinogen**, is converted to a fibrous protein called **fibrin**. This forms a mesh of fibres across the wound. Red blood cells and platelets get trapped in the mesh, forming a clot.

Plasma

Blood plasma is mostly water. It contains many dissolved substances that are being transported from one part of the body to another. These include:

- mineral ions (for example calcium ions);
- soluble nutrients (for example glucose, amino acids);
- hormones (for example adrenaline);
- carbon dioxide (a waste product of respiration).

Quick test

1. What is the function of valves in the circulatory system?
2. Where in the heart is the septum?
3. Name the type of blood vessel that transports blood away from the heart.
4. List **three** ways in which the activity of the heart can be monitored.
5. What is coronary heart disease?
6. Which type of blood vessel contains valves?
7. Name the component of blood that transports oxygen.

Supplement

8. Explain the advantages of a double circulatory system compared with a single circulatory system.
9. Why do arteries have elastic tissue in their walls?
10. List **two** components of the lymphatic system.

Diseases and immunity

Some diseases are caused by **pathogens**. These include bacteria, viruses and protoctists. Pathogens can be passed from one person to another, so diseases caused by a pathogen are **transmissible diseases**.

Definitions

Pathogen – a disease-causing organism.
Transmissible disease – a disease in which the pathogen can be passed from one host to another.

Transmission of pathogens

A pathogen may be transmitted by:

- direct contact, for example by one person's blood coming into contact with another person's blood;
- indirect contact, for example from contaminated surfaces or food, from animals, or by breathing air containing droplets of liquid sneezed out by someone with a respiratory infection.

Body defences

The body has defences to limit the ability of pathogens to get in, or to breed inside the body.

Mechanical barriers The skin is a tough, impenetrable barrier that most pathogens cannot get through. The hairs in the nose help to stop dust containing pathogens getting down into the lungs.

Chemical barriers The stomach produces hydrochloric acid, which kills many of the bacteria present in the food that we eat, or the water that we drink. Mucus in the trachea and bronchi helps to trap pathogens and stop them reaching the lungs.

White blood cells use phagocytosis and antibodies to destroy pathogens once they are inside the body.

Controlling the spread of disease

Vaccination helps to protect against transmissible diseases. This involves giving the body a dose of a weakened pathogen, so that the white blood cells 'learn' how to destroy that pathogen. Vaccination reduces the number of people in whom a pathogen can breed, so it reduces the spread of the disease.

Good **food hygiene** reduces the chance of pathogens entering the body in food. For example:

- Keep hands, tools and work surfaces clean, so that they cannot transfer pathogens to the food.
- Do not allow food to remain warm for long periods of time. Keep it cold (to slow down growth of bacteria) or very hot (to kill them).
- Keep cooked meat away from raw meat, so that no bacteria can be transferred from the raw meat.

Good **personal hygiene** reduces the chances of passing a pathogen from one person to another. For example:

- Wash hands frequently; never put your hands to your mouth until you have cleaned them. Be particularly careful to wash your hands after using the toilet, to avoid spreading pathogens from faeces.
- Do not cough or sneeze into the air or over another person.

Careful **waste disposal** reduces the opportunities for pathogens to breed in the waste. For example:

- Cover bins containing food waste, to prevent access by flies and rats.
- Ensure all waste is disposed of in proper landfill sites, where it will be covered by soil.

Sewage treatment reduces the chance of pathogens entering water bodies, in which people may later swim, or where they may drink the water. Raw sewage should not be allowed to flow into rivers, lakes or the sea.

Supplement

Antibodies

Antibodies are proteins that are produced by lymphocytes. Each lymphocyte only produces antibodies when it has come into contact with its specific antigen. An antigen is a molecule that is foreign to your own body. It may be on the surface of a pathogen, or it may be a toxin molecule that has been produced by a pathogen and is circulating in the blood.

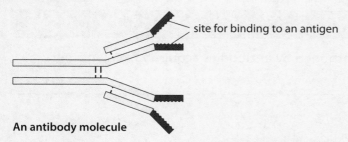

site for binding to an antigen

An antibody molecule

> **Revision tip**

Remember:
An anti**body** is produced by your own **body**.
An anti**gen** is produced by a patho**gen**.

> **Revision tip**

Antibodies are molecules, not cells. One white blood cell can produce millions of antibody molecules.

Each antibody molecule has a specifically shaped binding site that has a complementary shape to the antigen with which it can bind. Each antibody is therefore specific to a particular antigen.

When an antibody binds to its antigen it can:

- directly destroy the antigen, or the pathogen to which the antigen belongs;
- mark the antigen, so that phagocytes will come and destroy it by phagocytosis.

> **Revision tip**

Take care to say that an antibody has a complementary shape to its antigen, not 'the same shape'.

Immunity

Active immunity

When a lymphocyte first encounters its specific antigen, the lymphocyte divides over and over again to form a **clone** of cells just like itself. These cells then secrete large quantities of the specific antibody that binds with the antigen. This takes time. Meanwhile the pathogen breeds and makes you ill. Eventually, if enough antibodies are made, the pathogen is destroyed and you get better.

After this has happened, some of the lymphocytes become **memory cells**, which remain in the body for many years. If the same pathogen enters the body again, there will already be many cells that can produce the antibody against its antigens. It is likely that the pathogen will be destroyed before it can make you ill. You are **immune** to that disease.

Vaccination inserts a weakened pathogen, or its antigens, into your body. Your lymphocytes react just as they would to a normal pathogen, and memory cells are produced that make you immune. This is a way of becoming immune without having the disease.

Both of these methods produce **active immunity**. It is called active because you make your own antibodies. Active immunity lasts for a long time, because you have produced memory cells.

> ### Definition
>
> **Active immunity** – defence against a pathogen by antibody production in the body.

Vaccination is important in reducing the spread of disease. The more people in a population are vaccinated, the fewer places there are for the pathogen to breed. This reduces the chance of any unvaccinated people getting the disease.

Passive immunity

You can be given an injection of ready-made antibodies. These will destroy their specific antigen, but they do not remain in the body for very long.

Young babies also get ready-made antibodies in their mother's milk. This protects them against any disease to which their mothers have developed immunity. This is important because a young baby's own immune system takes some time to develop fully.

Both of these produce **passive immunity**. It is called passive because you simply receive antibodies from elsewhere, without your lymphocytes making them themselves. Passive immunity doesn't last very long, because you have not made memory cells.

> ### Definition
>
> **Passive immunity** – short-term defence against a pathogen by antibodies acquired from another individual, for example mother to infant.

Type 1 diabetes

Type 1 diabetes is an illness in which the cells in the pancreas that make insulin are destroyed. This disease is not caused by a pathogen. It is caused by the body's own lymphocytes behaving as though the pancreas cells are foreign, and attacking them as though they carry foreign antigens.

Quick test

1. Define the term *pathogen*.
2. Name one mechanical barrier that prevents the entry of pathogens to the body.
3. List two ways in which white blood cells help to protect against disease-causing organisms.
4. Explain why food should not be kept warm for long periods of time.

Supplement

5. What are antibodies, and how do they help to protect against disease?
6. Explain the difference between active immunity and passive immunity. Give an example of how each of these types of immunity can be achieved.
7. Name a disease that is caused by the immune system targeting body cells.

1 The diagram shows a section through the human heart.

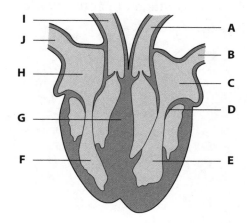

(a) Give the letter **and** name of each of the following:

   (i) a blood vessel that contains oxygenated blood;

   (ii) a chamber of the heart that contains deoxygenated blood;

   (iii) the chamber of the heart that pumps blood to the lungs;

   (iv) a blood vessel that transports oxygenated blood to the heart;

   (v) a structure that keeps blood flowing in the correct direction;

   (vi) a structure that keeps oxygenated blood separate from deoxygenated blood in the heart. [6]

(b) A woman is told that she is at risk of developing coronary heart disease.

   (i) Name the blood vessels that become blocked in coronary heart disease. [1]

   (ii) List **two** factors that increase the risk of developing coronary heart disease. [2]

Supplement

2 When a person does vigorous exercise, their heart rate increases. When exercise stops, the heart rate stays high for a while, and then steadily returns to normal.

   (a) Describe how you could measure a person's heart rate in a school laboratory. [2]

   (b) Explain why heart rate increases when a person does vigorous exercise. [5]

   (c) Explain why heart rate does not return to normal immediately, when the exercise stops. [4]

3 **(a) (i)** List **two** differences between the structure of arteries and veins. [2]

(ii) For each difference you have listed, explain the reason for the difference. [2]

(b) The graph shows the number of measles cases in the world between 1980 and 2009. It also shows the estimated percentage of people, worldwide, who were vaccinated against measles in each year.

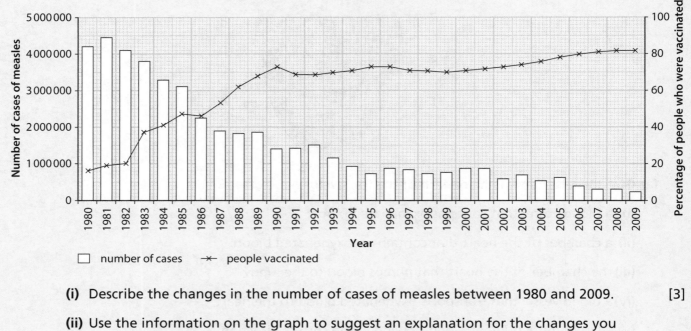

(i) Describe the changes in the number of cases of measles between 1980 and 2009. [3]

(ii) Use the information on the graph to suggest an explanation for the changes you have described in **(i)**. [3]

(c) Explain why immunity to measles does not provide immunity to other transmissible diseases. [3]

Gas exchange in humans

All living organisms respire. **Respiration** is a series of chemical reactions that takes place inside every living cell. Respiration oxidises glucose, releasing energy from the glucose molecules. You can find out more about respiration in the next section of this chapter.

In humans, respiration is normally **aerobic**. This means that is uses **oxygen**. Aerobic respiration produces **carbon dioxide**. Humans therefore need to take in oxygen, and remove carbon dioxide from the body. This is called **gas exchange**.

The human gas exchange system

In humans, gas exchange happens in the **alveoli** (singular: alveolus) in the **lungs**. Gas exchange happens by **diffusion**.

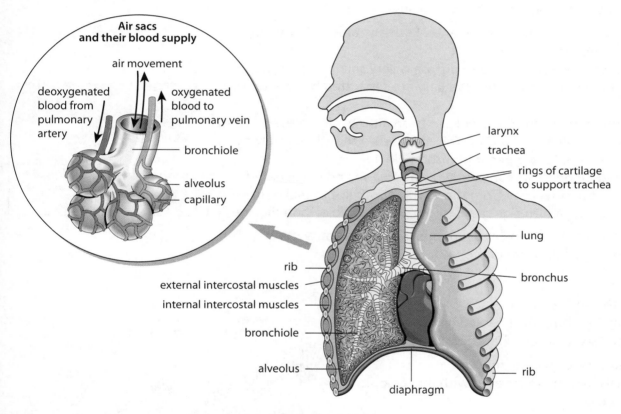

Air moves to and from the alveoli along the **trachea, bronchi** (singular: bronchus) and **bronchioles**.

Deoxygenated blood moves to the alveoli along capillaries that branch from the pulmonary artery.

Oxygenated blood moves from the alveoli along capillaries that join up to form the pulmonary vein.

The capillaries lie closely against the walls of the alveoli. Oxygen diffuses from the air inside the alveoli into the capillaries. It does this because the concentration of oxygen is higher inside the air in the alveoli than in the deoxygenated blood. There is therefore a diffusion gradient for oxygen, from the alveoli into the blood.

Carbon dioxide diffuses from the blood into the air inside the alveoli. It does this because the concentration of carbon dioxide is higher inside the deoxygenated blood than in the air inside the alveoli. There is therefore a diffusion gradient for carbon dioxide, from the blood into the alveoli.

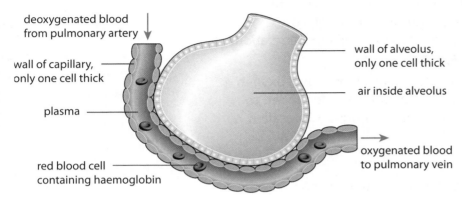

The alveoli are adapted for gas exchange because:

- They have a very large total surface area. Each alveolus is very small, but there are millions of them.
- The distance that the gases have to diffuse is very small. The air in the alveolus and the blood inside the capillary are separated by only two cells.
- Air moves into and out of the alveoli, so fresh air is always present. The air movement is called **ventilation**. This makes sure that there is always a diffusion gradient for oxygen and carbon dioxide.
- Deoxygenated blood flows constantly to the alveoli and oxygenated blood flows constantly away from them. This also helps to make sure that there is always a diffusion gradient for oxygen and carbon dioxide.

> **Revision tip**
>
> Do not say that there are thin 'cell walls' in the alveoli. These are animal cells, so they do not have cell walls. It is the walls of the alveolus and the walls of the capillary that are thin.

The inner surfaces of the alveoli are kept moist by a layer of watery mucus. This stops the cells from drying out.

Supplement

Protecting the lungs

The inner surface of the trachea and bronchi is covered with a layer of cells that contains:

- **goblet cells**, which secrete mucus
- **ciliated cells**, which are covered with microscopic 'hairs' called cilia.

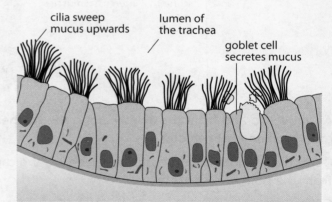

Bacteria and small particles in the air are trapped in the sticky mucus. The cilia wave in unison, pushing the mucus up towards the back of the throat where it is swallowed.

This helps to prevent bacteria (which could be pathogens) and small particles getting into the lungs, where they could cause damage.

Breathing movements

The movement of air into and out of the lungs is caused by **breathing movements**. Three sets of muscles are involved.

Breathing in is called **inspiration**.

- **Muscles in the diaphragm** contract, pulling the diaphragm downwards.
- The **external intercostal muscles** contract, pulling the ribs upwards.
- These both increase the volume inside the thorax (chest cavity).
- The pressure inside the thorax therefore decreases.
- Air from outside the body therefore flows into the thorax down the trachea, from the higher pressure outside the thorax to the lower pressure region inside it.

Breathing out is called **expiration**.

- Muscles in the diaphragm relax, allowing the diaphragm to spring upwards.
- The external intercostal muscles relax, allowing the ribs to drop downwards.
- These both decrease the volume inside the thorax (chest cavity).
- The pressure inside the thorax therefore increases.
- Air from inside the body therefore flows out of the thorax up the trachea, from the higher pressure inside the thorax to the lower pressure region outside it.

The **internal intercostal muscles** are used when you are breathing heavily. When they contract, they pull the ribcage downwards, decreasing the volume in the thorax. This helps to force air out of the lungs.

Event	Diaphragm muscles	External intercostal muscles	Internal intercostal muscles
inspiration	contract	contract	relax
expiration	relax	relax	contract

Comparing inspired air and expired air
The air around us is the air that we breathe in. This is **inspired air**. The air that we breathe out is **expired air**.
The table shows the composition of inspired air and expired air.

Gas	Percentage in inspired air	Percentage in expired air
oxygen	21	16
carbon dioxide	0.04	4
water vapour	varies	always high

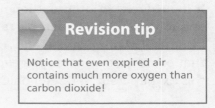

Revision tip

Notice that even expired air contains much more oxygen than carbon dioxide!

The apparatus in the diagram below can be used to compare the concentration of carbon dioxide in inspired air and expired air.

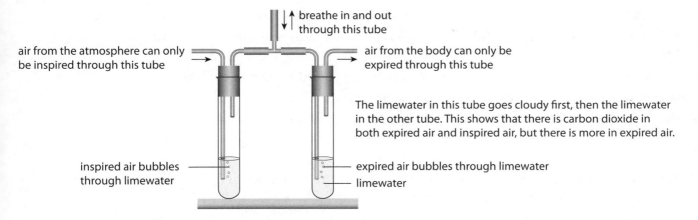

breathe in and out through this tube

air from the atmosphere can only be inspired through this tube

air from the body can only be expired through this tube

The limewater in this tube goes cloudy first, then the limewater in the other tube. This shows that there is carbon dioxide in both expired air and inspired air, but there is more in expired air.

inspired air bubbles through limewater

expired air bubbles through limewater

limewater

Expired air contains less oxygen than inspired air because oxygen is used in all the cells in the body in respiration.

Expired air contains more carbon dioxide than inspired air because carbon dioxide is produced in all the cells in the body in respiration.

Expired air always contains a lot of water vapour because water evaporates from the moist lining of the alveoli.

Effect of exercise on breathing rate

When you exercise, you breathe faster and deeper. This is so that you get more oxygen to your working muscles, and to remove the extra carbon dioxide that they produce during exercise.

A graph showing how breathing rate changes during and after exercise is very similar to the one on page 41, showing how heart rate changes during and after exercise.

When exercise begins:

- Muscles contract more frequently, which requires more energy.
- The muscle cells therefore respire faster, releasing more energy.
- For aerobic respiration, the muscles require oxygen, so their need for oxygen increases.
- The faster respiration produces more carbon dioxide, which dissolves in the blood plasma.
- The brain detects the increased carbon dioxide in the blood.
- The brain sends impulses along nerves to the diaphragm muscles and intercostal muscles, increasing the depth and rate of breathing movements.

If the exercise is intense, then not enough oxygen may be supplied to the muscles to allow them to get enough energy from aerobic respiration alone. They therefore also respire anaerobically. This produces lactic acid. After exercise ends, the lactic acid is broken down by combining it with oxygen. This means that extra oxygen is needed even after exercise has ended, so breathing rate continues to be high until this oxygen debt has been paid off.

Quick test

1. Name the gas exchange surface in humans.
2. List **four** features of this gas exchange surface that help gas exchange to take place efficiently.
3. List, in the correct order, the tubes through which air passes as it moves from outside the body to the gas exchange surface.
4. List **three** differences between the composition of inspired air and expired air.
5. Name a substance that is used to test for carbon dioxide.
6. Describe **two** ways in which breathing changes during physical activity.

7. Summarise what happens to (a) volume and (b) pressure inside the lungs during breathing in (inspiration) and breathing out (expiration).
8. Describe the roles of the external and internal intercostal muscles during breathing.
9. Describe where goblet cells and ciliated cells are found, and explain their functions.

Respiration is a series of metabolic reactions that takes place in every living cell. Like all metabolic reactions, they are controlled by enzymes.

Respiration releases energy from glucose. In humans, this energy is used for:

- **muscle contraction**, which causes movement
- **building protein molecules** by linking together amino acids
- **cell division**, which is important for **growth**
- sending **electrical impulses** along neurones (nerve cells)
- keeping the **body temperature** constant
- **active transport** of substances into and out of cells.

Aerobic respiration

'Aerobic' means 'using air'. It is actually oxygen from air that is used.

Definition

Aerobic respiration – the chemical reactions in cells that use oxygen to break down nutrient molecules to release energy.

The word equation for aerobic respiration is:

glucose + oxygen $\longrightarrow$ carbon dioxide + water

Supplement

The balanced chemical equation for respiration is:

$$C_6H_{12}O_6 + 6O_2 \longrightarrow 6CO_2 + 6H_2O$$

The apparatus in the diagram can be used to investigate the rate of uptake of oxygen by small respiring organisms. This tells us how quickly they are respiring.

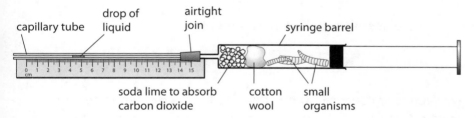

- As the organisms respire aerobically, they take in oxygen and give out carbon dioxide in approximately equal volumes.
- The carbon dioxide is absorbed by the soda lime.
- The volume of air inside the syringe barrel therefore decreases.
- This causes the drop of liquid to move along the capillary tube towards the organisms.
- The faster the rate of respiration, the faster the drop of liquid moves along the capillary tube.

The apparatus can be used to compare the rate of respiration of small organisms, for example germinating seeds, at different temperatures.

The apparatus is set up and kept in the first chosen temperature for 10 minutes, to allow the organisms to adjust.

The position of the drop of liquid is recorded at suitable time intervals, for example every 5 minutes. The mean rate of respiration is then calculated by dividing the total distance moved by the total time taken.

This is then repeated at different temperatures. It is important to keep all other variables (for example mass of organisms, initial composition of air inside the syringe barrel) constant.

Anaerobic respiration

'An' means 'without', so anaerobic respiration is respiration without oxygen.

Definition

Anaerobic respiration – the chemical reactions in cells that break down nutrient molecules to release energy without using oxygen.

Anaerobic respiration releases much less energy from each glucose molecule than aerobic respiration. Human body cells therefore only use anaerobic respiration when they are short of oxygen.

There are two types of anaerobic respiration:

- In humans, anaerobic respiration produces **lactic acid**.

    glucose $\longrightarrow$ lactic acid

- In yeast and plants, anaerobic respiration produces **alcohol** and **carbon dioxide**.

    glucose $\longrightarrow$ alcohol + carbon dioxide

The balanced chemical equation for the anaerobic respiration in yeast and plants is:

$$C_6H_{12}O_6 \longrightarrow 2C_2H_5OH + 2CO_2$$

Oxygen debt

When we do vigorous exercise, we have seen that contracting muscles need more oxygen to release more energy by aerobic respiration. Heart rate and breathing rate increase in order to supply this extra oxygen to the working muscles.

However, this extra oxygen still may not be enough to allow the muscles to release all the energy that they need. The muscle cells therefore top up the energy release by using anaerobic respiration as well.

The lactic acid that is produced by anaerobic respiration builds up in the muscle cells. It diffuses into the blood, and is transported to the liver. The faster heart rate helps to speed up this transport.

Liver cells break down the lactic acid by combining it with oxygen, in aerobic respiration. This continues after the exercise has finished. This means that extra oxygen continues to be required for some minutes afterwards. This is called an **oxygen debt**. The extra oxygen is supplied to the liver cells by faster breathing and a faster heart rate, both of which continue for some time after exercising has finished.

Quick test

1. Define *aerobic respiration*.
2. Write the word equation for aerobic respiration.
3. Explain why it is important not to say that respiration 'produces' energy.
4. In which body cells does aerobic respiration happen?
5. List **two** differences between aerobic respiration and anaerobic respiration in humans.
6. State one difference between anaerobic respiration in humans and anaerobic respiration in yeast.

Supplement

7. Write the balanced chemical equation for aerobic respiration.
8. Write the balanced chemical equation for anaerobic respiration in yeast.
9. Explain where and why anaerobic respiration takes place in humans.
10. Explain why we continue to breathe faster and deeper for some time after exercise finishes.

Excretion

We have seen that carbon dioxide is produced in aerobic respiration, and is removed by the lungs. This is an example of **excretion**. Excretion is the removal of the waste products of metabolism, or substances in excess of requirements, from the body.

In humans:

- **carbon dioxide** produced in respiration is excreted through the lungs;
- **urea** produced in the liver, from excess amino acids, is excreted through the kidneys;
- **excess salts** and **excess water** are excreted through the kidneys.

The liquid produced by the kidneys is called **urine**. It flows down through the two **ureters**, is stored in the **bladder**, and leaves the body through the **urethra**.

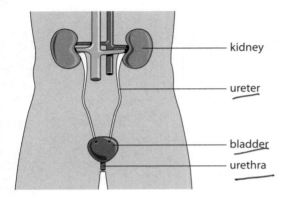

The volume and concentration of the urine produced by the kidneys is affected by:

- how much liquid you have drunk; the more water you have taken in, the more urine will be produced;
- how hot it is, or how much exercise you do; the hotter you are, the more water you will lose in sweat, so the less water will be lost in urine.

Supplement

Roles of the liver

Protein in foods that you eat is digested to amino acids in the alimentary canal. These amino acids are transported to the liver in the blood in the hepatic portal vein.

In the liver:

- some of the amino acids are built into proteins, such as the plasma protein fibrinogen;
- amino acids in excess of the body's needs are broken down to urea. This is called **deamination**.

Definition

Deamination – the removal of the nitrogen-containing part of amino acids to form urea.

Urea, like carbon dioxide, is toxic – that is, it would harm body cells if too much accumulated in the body. It is therefore important that it is removed.

Roles of the kidneys

The diagrams show the structure and functions of the kidneys. Each kidney contains thousands of tiny tubules called **nephrons**, which produce urine.

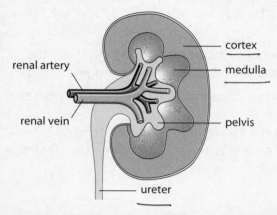

renal artery

cortex

medulla

renal vein

pelvis

ureter

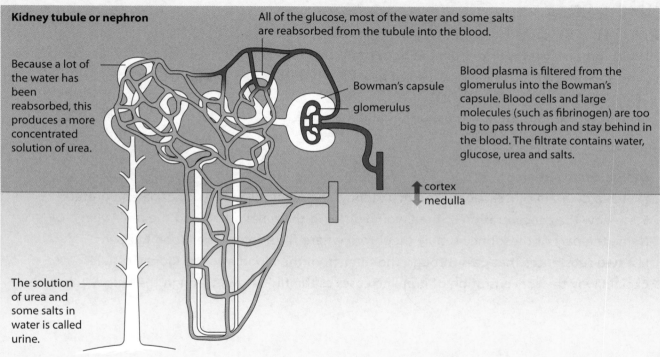

Kidney tubule or nephron

All of the glucose, most of the water and some salts are reabsorbed from the tubule into the blood.

Because a lot of the water has been reabsorbed, this produces a more concentrated solution of urea.

Bowman's capsule

glomerulus

Blood plasma is filtered from the glomerulus into the Bowman's capsule. Blood cells and large molecules (such as fibrinogen) are too big to pass through and stay behind in the blood. The filtrate contains water, glucose, urea and salts.

cortex
medulla

The solution of urea and some salts in water is called urine.

Dialysis

If kidneys stop working, urea and other toxins build up in the blood and cause severe health problems. The person can be treated using **dialysis**.

Dialysis involves passing the person's blood through a machine in which the blood is separated from dialysis fluid by a partially permeable membrane.

The dialysis fluid contains water, salts and glucose. The concentration of glucose and salts in the fluid is the concentration that is ideal in human blood. The dialysis fluid does not contain any urea.

As the blood flows through the machine:

- urea diffuses through the membrane out of the blood and into the dialysis fluid, down its concentration gradient;
- glucose diffuses either into or out of the blood, depending on whether its concentration in the blood is lower or higher than in the dialysis fluid;
- water moves by osmosis either into or out of the blood, depending on whether the water potential of the blood is lower or higher than in the dialysis fluid.

Dialysis works well, but it has disadvantages:

- dialysis machines are expensive and require well-trained operators to maintain them;
- the person has to be linked up to the machine regularly, for several hours at a time;
- in between treatments, the concentrations of urea and other toxic substances in the blood will build up and may damage body tissues.

An alternative is for the patient to have a **kidney transplant**. The big advantage of this is that – if the transplant is successful – no further treatment is needed. However, this also has disadvantages:

- Kidneys for transplants are in short supply. The kidney must be a close match to the person's own cell types, or the immune system will reject it.
- Even if the cell types are a good match, the person receiving the kidney will probably need to take immunosuppressant drugs for the rest of their life. This can leave them more vulnerable to infectious diseases.

Quick test

1. Where is urea formed, and what is it formed from?
2. Which organ excretes urea from the body?
3. A person does a lot of exercise on a hot day. What effect would this have on the volume and concentration of the urine they produce?
4. Explain the difference between a ureter and a urethra.

Supplement

5. Define *deamination*.
6. Sketch a diagram of a section through a kidney, and label the cortex, medulla and ureter.
7. State how the concentration of urea would differ in the renal artery and the renal vein.
8. Name the part of the kidney tubule (nephron) where filtration of the blood happens.
9. List **two** substances that pass through the filter from the blood into the kidney tubule.
10. Explain why the concentration of urea increases as the fluid flows through the kidney tubule.

1 **(a)** Respiration is a series of reactions that releases energy from nutrients such as glucose.

    (i) List **two** uses of energy in human body cells. [2]

    (ii) Complete the word equation for **aerobic** respiration.

    .... + ... ⟶ carbon dioxide + ... [2]

    (iii) Describe **two** ways in which anaerobic respiration differs from aerobic respiration. [2]

  (b) Carbon dioxide is an excretory product.

    (i) Define the term *excretion*. [2]

    (ii) Describe how carbon dioxide is removed from the body. [3]

  (c) Urea is also an excretory product.

    (i) Name the organ where urea is formed. [1]

    (ii) Name the substances from which urea is formed. [1]

    (iii) Name the organ that excretes urea from the body. [1]

Supplement

2 **(a)** Write the balanced chemical equation for aerobic respiration. [2]

  (b) The diagram shows apparatus that can be used to investigate the rate of respiration of germinating seeds.

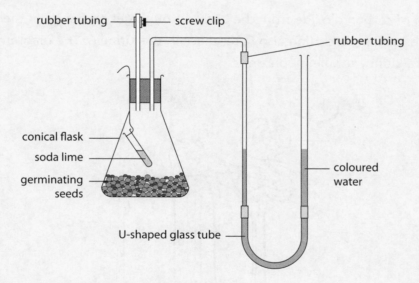

    (i) Explain the function of the soda lime. [2]

    (ii) Describe **and** explain what happens to the level of the coloured water in the U-shaped tube, as the germinating seeds respire. [4]

    (iii) A student used this apparatus to investigate the effect of temperature on the rate of respiration of germinating seeds.

The table shows her results.

Temperature (°C)	Difference between levels of fluid in the two arms of the tube (mm)			
	First try	Second try	Third try	Mean
0	2	1	2	1.3
10	4	4	5	4.3
20	12	14	13	13.0
30	23	28	25	
40	32	31	34	

Complete the table by calculating the mean values for 30 °C and 40 °C. [1]

(iv) List **two** variables that the student should have kept the same in her investigation. [2]

(v) The student concluded that the optimum temperature for respiration in germinating seeds is 40 °C. Explain why this is not a valid conclusion. [2]

(vi) Explain the pattern shown in the student's results. [4]

3 **(a)** Several sets of muscles are involved in ventilation of the lungs. Complete the sentences to describe what happens during **inspiration**.

When you breathe in, the .... muscles and the .... muscles .... This increases the .... inside the thorax, and decreases the .... Air is drawn into the lungs down the trachea. [5]

(b) Gas exchange takes place between the alveoli in the lungs, and the blood.

(i) Explain how ventilation helps to increase the rate of gas exchange. [2]

(ii) Explain how **two** other features of the alveoli help to increase the rate of gas exchange. [4]

(c) The removal of carbon dioxide from the body, through gas exchange in the lungs, is an example of excretion. Excretion also takes place in the kidneys. The diagram shows the structure of a kidney tubule (nephron).

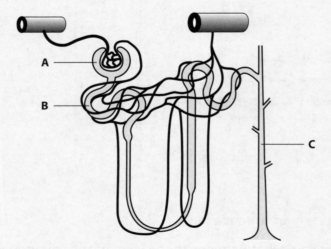

(i) Give the **letter** of the part of the kidney tubule where filtration of the blood takes place. [1]

(ii) Explain why the concentration of urea in the fluid inside the tubule increases as the fluid flows from **A** to **C**. [2]

Nervous control in humans

Information is carried rapidly from one part of the human body to another in the form of electrical signals passing along specialised cells called **neurones**.

This transfer of information between different parts of the body helps to **coordinate** their actions.

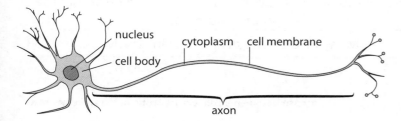

Neurones are nerve cells. They are found in the **nervous system**. This is made up of two parts:

- the **central nervous system**, which includes the **brain** and the **spinal cord**;
- the **peripheral nervous system**, which includes the **nerves** that carry impulses to and from other parts of the body.

The diagram shows how information can be transferred very rapidly between a **receptor** and an **effector**.

- Receptors are found in sense organs, and respond to changes in the external environment. These changes are called **stimuli** (singular: stimulus).
- Effectors are parts of the body that respond to a stimulus. Muscles and glands are effectors.

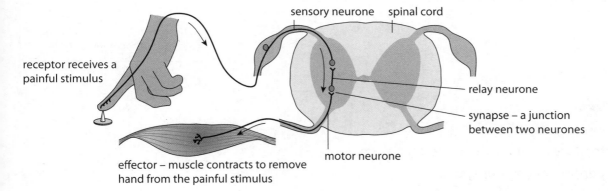

The pathway shown in the diagram is called a **reflex arc**.

The type of response to a stimulus shown in the diagram is called a **reflex action**. It is a very rapid, automatic response, which does not involve any decision-making by the brain. Reflex arcs are a means of coordinating stimuli with the responses of effectors (muscles and glands).

Definition

Synapse – a junction between two neurones.

Revision tip

Do not say that neurones carry 'messages'. It is better to say that they carry electrical signals or electrical impulses.

Revision tip

A nerve cell or neurone is not the same as a nerve. A nerve is made up of hundreds or thousands of neurones.

Most of our actions are not reflex actions. Normally, we make decisions about the actions that we take. These are **voluntary actions**. Reflex actions are **involuntary actions**.

Voluntary action	Involuntary action
Involves a conscious decision made in cerebral hemispheres of the brain.	Involves only the spinal cord or other parts of the brain.
Relatively slow.	Faster.
The same stimulus can produce a variety of different responses.	The same stimulus always produces the same response; the response is automatic.
Many voluntary actions are learnt.	Many involuntary actions are instinctive.

Synapses

A synapse is a very tiny gap between two neurones.

When a nerve impulse arrives at the end of the sensory neurone:

- vesicles containing neurotransmitters move to the cell membrane of the sensory neurone;
- the vesicles burst open and empty the neurotransmitter into the synaptic cleft;
- the neurotransmitter diffuses across the cleft;
- the neurotransmitter molecules slot into their receptors on the membrane of the relay neurone;
- this sets off a nerve impulse in the relay neurone.

A synapse between a sensory neurone and a relay neurone

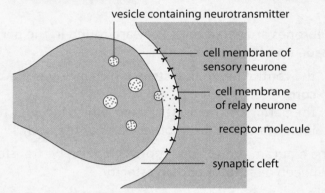

vesicle containing neurotransmitter

cell membrane of sensory neurone

cell membrane of relay neurone

receptor molecule

synaptic cleft

A nerve impulse can travel in only one direction along the reflex arc, because the neurotransmitter is present on only one side of the synapse.

Many drugs, including heroin, act at synapses. This is described later in this chapter.

> **Revision tip**
>
> The receptor molecules have a complementary shape to the neurotransmitter molecules, so that they fit together perfectly.

Quick test

1. What is a nerve impulse?
2. Name **two** structures that make up the central nervous system.
3. What is the peripheral nervous system?
4. List, in order, the three neurones along which a nerve impulse travels in a reflex arc.
5. Use the diagram of a reflex arc to describe **one** difference between the structure of a sensory neurone and a motor neurone.

Supplement

6. List **two** differences between voluntary and involuntary actions.
7. Explain why a nerve impulse can pass in only one direction along a reflex arc.
8. A student wrote that neurotransmitter molecules and their receptor molecules at a synapse are the same shape. What is wrong with this statement?

The eye

The eye is an example of a sense organ.

> ### Definition
>
> **Sense organs** – groups of receptor cells responding to specific stimuli:
> light, sound, touch, temperature and chemicals.

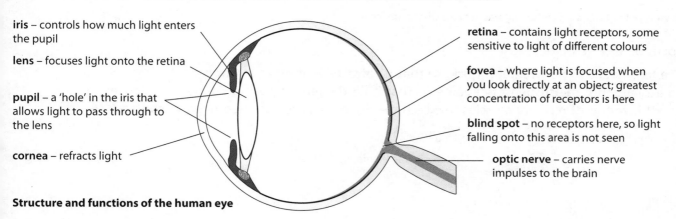

iris – controls how much light enters the pupil

lens – focuses light onto the retina

pupil – a 'hole' in the iris that allows light to pass through to the lens

cornea – refracts light

retina – contains light receptors, some sensitive to light of different colours

fovea – where light is focused when you look directly at an object; greatest concentration of receptors is here

blind spot – no receptors here, so light falling onto this area is not seen

optic nerve – carries nerve impulses to the brain

Structure and functions of the human eye

- Light enters the eye through the cornea.
- Light is refracted (bent) as it passes through the cornea and the lens.
- Light is focused onto the receptor cells in the retina.
- This sets off nerve impulses that travel along the optic nerve to the brain.

The pupil reflex

If the light is very bright, it may damage the retina. Muscles in the iris contract, making the diameter of the pupil smaller so that less light can enter the eye. This is a reflex action.

> ### Supplement
>
> When intense light falls onto the retina, impulses pass along sensory neurones to the brain, and then along motor neurones to the muscles in the iris.
>
> This causes circular muscles in the iris to contract, which makes them shorter, so that the diameter of the pupil is decreased. This reduces the amount of light that passes through the pupil.
>
> In dim light, a similar reflex action results in the contraction of radial muscles in the iris. This widens the pupil, allowing more light into the eye.
>
> The actions of the radial and circular muscles are said to be antagonistic. They have opposite effects. When one set of muscles contracts, the other relaxes.
>
>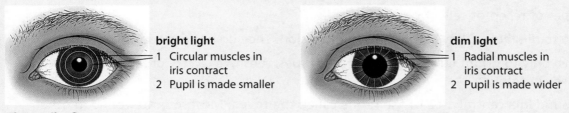
>
> **bright light**
> 1 Circular muscles in iris contract
> 2 Pupil is made smaller
>
> **dim light**
> 1 Radial muscles in iris contract
> 2 Pupil is made wider
>
> **The pupil reflex**

Accommodation

Accommodation is the changes that take place in the eye to focus on objects at different distances.

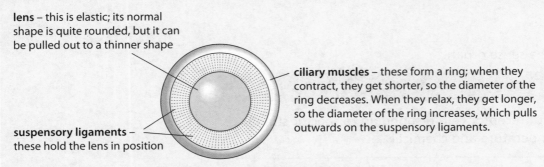

lens – this is elastic; its normal shape is quite rounded, but it can be pulled out to a thinner shape

ciliary muscles – these form a ring; when they contract, they get shorter, so the diameter of the ring decreases. When they relax, they get longer, so the diameter of the ring increases, which pulls outwards on the suspensory ligaments.

suspensory ligaments – these hold the lens in position

Front view of the lens, suspensory ligaments and ciliary muscles

To focus on a close object:

- the lens needs to be **wide** and **thick**, so that it refracts light **more strongly**;
- to achieve this, the suspensory ligaments that hold the lens in position need to be **loose**;
- to achieve this, the ciliary muscles to which the ligaments are attached need to **contract**.

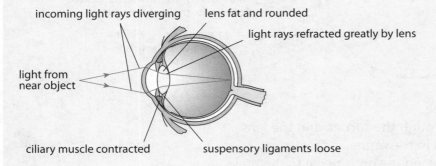

incoming light rays diverging

lens fat and rounded

light rays refracted greatly by lens

light from near object

ciliary muscle contracted

suspensory ligaments loose

To focus on a distant object:

- the lens needs to be **narrow** and **thin**, so that it refracts light **less strongly**;
- to achieve this, the suspensory ligaments must be **pulled tight**;
- to achieve this, the ciliary muscles need to **relax**.

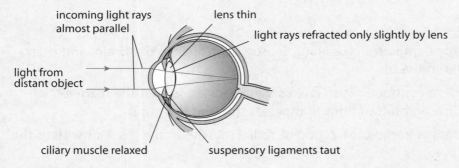

incoming light rays almost parallel

lens thin

light rays refracted only slightly by lens

light from distant object

ciliary muscle relaxed

suspensory ligaments taut

The retina

The retina is the tissue at the back of the eye that contains cells receptive to light.

There are two types of receptor cell.

Rods are sensitive to dim light. They are used for night vision. They do not provide colour vision.

Cones are sensitive only to bright light. There are three types, sensitive to red, green and blue light. This allows us to see in colour.

Most cones are found in a central area of the retina called the **fovea**. Most rods are found in other parts of the retina. The fovea is where light is focused when we look directly at an object.

Quick test

1. Put these parts of the eye in the order through which light passes:
   lens, pupil, cornea
2. Name the part of the eye that contains receptor cells that are sensitive to light.
3. What is the function of the optic nerve?
4. What is the blind spot?
5. Explain what happens to the diameter of the pupil in dim light.

Supplement

6. Which muscles contract to make the diameter of the pupil smaller?
7. Which muscles contract to make the lens become thicker and rounder?
8. Under what circumstances does this happen?
9. What is the fovea?
10. Compare the functions of rods and cones.

Hormones in humans

Hormones are chemicals that are produced by various **endocrine glands**. They are transported to all parts of the body dissolved in the blood plasma. Each hormone affects one or more **target organs**.

> **Definition**
>
> **Hormone** – a chemical substance, produced by a gland and carried by the blood, which alters the activity of one or more specific target organs.

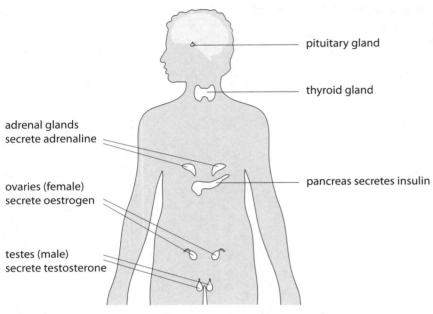

The positions of some endocrine glands in the human body

Hormone	Gland that secretes it	When secreted	Function
adrenaline	adrenal glands	when you are frightened or excited	increases breathing rate; increases pulse rate; widens pupils. This is called the fight or flight response.
insulin	pancreas	when blood glucose concentration is too high	causes liver to reduce the concentration of glucose in the blood
testosterone	testes	from puberty onwards	produces male secondary sexual characteristics
oestrogen	ovaries	from puberty onwards	produces female secondary sexual characteristics; helps to regulate the menstrual cycle

Adrenaline is involved in the chemical control of metabolic activity. It helps to prepare the body for vigorous action. It does this by:

- Causing the concentration of glucose in the blood to increase. This provides more fuel for respiration, so that muscle cells can release more energy to use for contraction. This could help with fleeing from a predator, or fighting it.
- Causing the pulse rate to increase. This increases the rate at which oxygen and glucose are delivered to muscles, so that they can respire faster and release more energy.

In general:

- Hormones act more slowly than nervous impulses. This is because hormones travel to their target organs in the blood, whereas nervous impulses travel very swiftly along neurones as electrical signals.
- Hormones act for a longer time than nervous impulses. This is because hormones remain in the blood for a while before they are broken down, whereas nervous impulses only happen at an instant in time.

Quick test

1. Define a *hormone*.
2. Name the gland that secretes insulin.
3. State the function of insulin.
4. Give one example of a situation where adrenaline would be secreted.

Supplement

5. Explain **two** effects of adrenaline on the body.
6. List **two** differences between nervous and hormonal control.

Homeostasis

Homeostasis means keeping conditions in the body as constant as possible. This enables cells to work efficiently.

The skin helps to keep the internal temperature of the body constant.

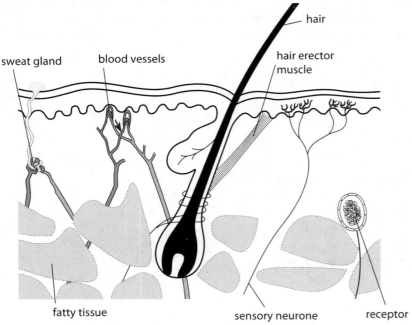

The structure of the skin of a mammal

The fatty layer beneath the skin helps to **insulate** the body, preventing heat loss.

The brain coordinates responses to changes in temperature. If internal body temperature rises too high:

- Blood temperature receptors in the brain detect the rise in temperature.
- This causes the brain to send nerve impulses to the sweat glands.
- This makes the sweat glands secrete more sweat, which evaporates and cools the skin.
- The erector muscles relax so hairs lie flat.

If internal body temperature falls too low:

- Blood temperature receptors in the brain detect the fall in temperature.
- This makes the brain send nerve impulses to the erector muscles and skeletal muscles.
- This makes the erector muscles contract so hairs are pulled erect, trapping an insulating layer of air.
- The skeletal muscles contract and relax quickly (shivering), releasing heat that helps to warm the blood.

Supplement

Blood vessels in the skin also help to regulate body temperature. Arterioles that supply blood to capillaries near the skin surface can become narrower (**vasoconstriction**) or wider (**vasodilation**).

If the arterioles become narrower, less blood is delivered to the surface capillaries, and blood is diverted beneath the fat layer. This reduces heat loss from the blood to the air.

If the arterioles become wider, more blood flows through the surface capillaries. More heat can therefore be lost to the air from the blood.

Negative feedback

Negative feedback is a mechanism that helps to keep a varying factor within set limits.

Negative feedback involves:

- a **receptor** that detects a change in a factor, for example a rise in blood temperature;
- an **effector** that responds to the change by bringing the factor back towards normal, for example by lowering the blood temperature.

Control of blood glucose concentration

It is important to keep blood glucose concentration within set limits. Glucose is needed by cells for the release of energy by respiration. If blood glucose concentration falls too low, cells may run short of energy. If its concentration rises too high, this reduces the water potential of the blood, so that water may move out of cells down the water potential gradient. Cells may become short of water, which damages them.

When blood glucose concentration rises too high:

- the pancreas secretes the hormone **insulin** into the blood;
- insulin is carried in the blood to the liver;
- insulin stimulates the liver to take up glucose from the blood;
- the liver changes glucose into the polysaccharide glycogen, and stores it.

When blood glucose concentration falls too low:

- The pancreas secretes the hormone **glucagon** into the blood.
- Glucagon is carried in the blood to the liver.
- Glucagon stimulates the liver to break down glycogen into glucose.
- The liver releases glucose into the blood.

Type 1 diabetes

In some people, their own immune system attacks and destroys the cells in the pancreas that secrete insulin. This results in **type 1 diabetes**.

After a meal, a person with type 1 diabetes may have blood glucose concentrations that rise much higher than normal. This is because there is no insulin to stimulate the liver to convert the extra glucose in the blood into glycogen.

Between meals, the blood glucose concentration may fall much lower than usual. The body cells gradually use up glucose in respiration. But there is little or no glycogen in the liver to be converted to glucose to top up the glucose concentration in the blood.

Some of the symptoms of diabetes are:

- feeling very thirsty; this happens because a high concentration of glucose in the blood decreases its water potential; the brain perceives this as meaning you need more water in the body;

- having glucose in the urine; this happens when blood glucose concentration rises so high that the kidneys are unable to absorb all the glucose back into the blood;
- blurred vision; this happens because the changes of concentration (water potential) of the blood cause osmosis to occur, which can change the shape of the lens in the eye;
- feeling very tired between meals; this happens when the blood glucose concentration drops very low, as there is not enough glucose to provide energy to cells through respiration.

If blood glucose levels rise extremely high, or fall extremely low, the person may go into a diabetic coma. This is a life-threatening condition.

Type 1 diabetes is treated with a combination of diet and insulin injections.

- The person needs to eat regular, small meals, to try to even out their intake of carbohydrate through the day. The quantity that they need will depend on the level of activity that they do.
- They can inject insulin after a meal, to reduce any 'spikes' in the blood glucose concentration.

Quick test

1. Define *homeostasis*.
2. State the function of the fat layer under the skin in regulating body temperature.
3. Describe how sweat glands help to regulate body temperature.

Supplement

4. Explain what is meant by negative feedback.
5. Which gland secretes glucagon?
6. Outline the function of glucagon.
7. List **two** symptoms of type 1 diabetes.
8. Describe how type 1 diabetes can be treated.

Plants can respond to stimuli by changing their direction of growth. These responses are called **tropisms**.

Definitions

Gravitropism – a response in which parts of a plant grow towards or away from gravity.

Phototropism – a response in which parts of a plant grow towards or away from the direction from which light is coming.

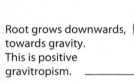

Root grows downwards, towards gravity. This is positive gravitropism.

Shoot grows upwards, away from gravity. This is negative gravitropism.

Gravitropism in a seedling

In even light, a shoot grows straight upwards.

In light from one side, a shoot grows towards the light. This is positive phototropism.

In darkness, a shoot grows very tall and spindly, and loses its green colour.

Responses by shoots to different lighting conditions

Supplement

A chemical called **auxin** helps to control tropisms. This is an example of the chemical control of plant growth.

Auxin is a plant hormone. It is made in the tips of shoots. It diffuses from the tip to other parts of the shoot.

Auxin stimulates cells to get longer. It does this by making them take up extra water.

When light is shining from one side of a plant shoot, active transport causes auxin to accumulate on the shady side. So the cells on the shady side elongate more than the cells on the bright side, and the shoot curves towards the light. If a shoot is growing horizontally, auxin accumulates on the lower side. This causes elongation of that side, so the shoot curves upwards.

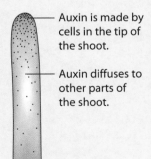

Auxin is made by cells in the tip of the shoot.

Auxin diffuses to other parts of the shoot.

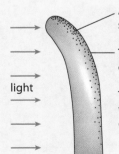

light

Auxin concentrates on the shady side of the shoot.

The high concentration of auxin causes cells to elongate.

The shady side elongates more than the bright side, so the shoot curves towards the light.

Phototropism in shoots

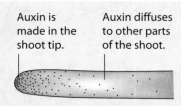

Auxin is made in the shoot tip.

Auxin diffuses to other parts of the shoot.

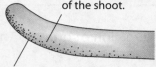

Auxin concentrates on the underside of the shoot.

The high concentration of auxin causes cells to elongate.

The underside elongates more than the bright side, so the shoot curves away from gravity.

Gravitropism in shoots

Quick test

1. Roots tend to grow away from light. What is the name for this response?
2. Suggest how phototropism helps a plant to make more glucose.

Supplement

3. What is auxin?
4. Where is auxin made?
5. How does auxin affect cells?
6. Explain how auxin makes a shoot grow towards light.

A **drug** is anything that you take into your body which affects the way that the body works.

Definition
Drug – a substance taken into the body that modifies or affects chemical reactions in the body.

Medicinal drugs

Medicinal drugs are drugs that help to prevent or cure diseases.

Antibiotics are drugs that kill bacteria inside the body. They are used to cure infections that are caused by pathogenic bacteria.

Some types of bacteria have become **resistant** to some kinds of antibiotics. This means that the antibiotics do not kill the bacteria.

Revision tip

Antibiotics only kill bacteria, not viruses.

Supplement

The more that bacteria are exposed to antibiotics, the more likely that resistant populations of bacteria will develop. This is explained in the section on natural selection on page 110. For example, some populations of a common bacterium called *Staphylococcus aureus* have become resistant to the antibiotic methicillin. They are known as methicillin-resistant *S. aureus*, or MRSA.

We can reduce the risk of bacteria developing resistance to antibiotics by reducing the use of antibiotics. For example, people should not be given antibiotics to cure things that they are not effective against, such as viral infections. It is also important for a person to take the complete course of antibiotics.

Revision tips

- Antibiotics do not destroy viruses, because antibiotics act against parts of bacterial cells that are not present in viruses – such as cell walls.
- Make sure you understand that it is bacteria that become resistant to antibiotics, not the person taking the antibiotic.

Misused drugs

Alcohol

Alcohol is a drug that has many effects.

- It is a **depressant**, meaning that it slows down nerve impulses and brain activity.
- This means that reaction times become longer, and self-control is reduced.
- Some people become **addicted** to alcohol. This means that they become unable to function normally without it. They may experience unpleasant **withdrawal symptoms** (such as nausea and tremors) if they do not continue to take it.
- People who are affected by alcohol may behave in antisocial ways, such as becoming aggressive.

Alcohol is broken down by cells in the liver. Excessive alcohol consumption over a long period of time damages the liver.

Heroin

Heroin is an opiate drug, obtained from opium poppies. Like alcohol, heroin is a depressant. It reduces pain and slows breathing rate. Addiction can develop quickly. A person who is addicted to heroin may lose their job and be unable to contribute to family life. They may turn to crime to get money to buy heroin.

A person who has become addicted to heroin may feel they need to take more and more of it. They may begin to inject it directly into the blood. This carries a large risk of transmitting a pathogen into the blood, such as HIV. See page 91 for more information about this.

Supplement

Heroin affects synapses in the brain. It fits into receptors that normally accept neurotransmitters called endorphins. Endorphins in the brain normally make us feel good. Heroin reduces the production of endorphins. If a person has been taking heroin, then they will have fewer endorphins, so there is nothing to fit into the endorphin receptors when they do not take heroin. They feel awful, suffering unpleasant withdrawal symptoms.

Nicotine

Nicotine is a drug that is found in tobacco smoke. People become addicted to nicotine, which makes it very difficult to give up smoking.

Cigarette smoke contains:

- **Carbon monoxide**. This combines with haemoglobin in the red blood cells even more readily than oxygen. This reduces the ability of the blood to transport oxygen.
- **Nicotine**. This addictive drug is absorbed into the blood and transported all over the body. It is a **stimulant**, making a person more alert. It causes damage to the circulatory system, and increases the risk of developing aneurisms (where arteries become wider, with thin walls that can easily burst open) and coronary heart disease.
- **Tar**. Tar is a mixture of many different substances. Some of these are **carcinogens**, which means that they increase the risk of developing cancer. People who smoke are more likely to develop many different kinds of cancer, including lung cancer.

Tobacco smoking also causes **chronic obstructive pulmonary disease, COPD**. This happens when the delicate walls of the alveoli break down, so that gas exchange cannot occur efficiently. The person cannot get enough oxygen into their blood, so their cells cannot release enough energy by respiration. Eventually they may not even have the energy to walk around, and need to lie or sit all day, perhaps breathing from an oxygen cylinder.

Supplement

The link between smoking and lung cancer was first discovered in the 1950s. Until then, no one realised that smoking harmed your health. The first evidence for the link was that the number of people getting lung cancer was steadily going up, running about 15 to 20 years behind an increase in the number of people smoking.

However, a **correlation** such as this does not prove that one thing is causing the other. It was some time before everyone accepted that smoking does indeed cause lung cancer. This has been shown by experiments in laboratories in which cells have been exposed to chemicals in cigarette smoke. This causes changes in their DNA, which lead to the cells dividing uncontrollably and forming cancerous tumours.

Anabolic steroids

The hormones testosterone, oestrogen and progesterone belong to a class of substances called **steroids**.

Testosterone is an **anabolic** steroid. An anabolic substance is one that stimulates metabolic reactions that result in muscle development and increased strength.

Some athletes have been tempted to take synthetic anabolic steroids to make them stronger, more aggressive and able to compete more successfully. Most sports now have rigorous testing regimes to detect this misuse of drugs. Besides being unfair on other competitors, taking anabolic steroids can cause severe harm to the body.

Quick test

1. Define the term *drug*.
2. What are antibiotics used for?
3. Which of these drugs are stimulants, and which are depressants?
   (a) Heroin.
   (b) Nicotine.
   (c) Alcohol.
4. Which organ breaks down toxins such as alcohol?
5. Which component of tobacco smoke increases the risk of lung cancer?
6. What is COPD?

Supplement

7. Explain how heroin affects the brain.
8. There is a correlation between smoking and lung cancer. What is meant by a correlation?
9. Explain why some athletes take anabolic steroids.

1 **(a)** The diagram shows a reflex arc. This is a pathway along which electrical impulses pass during a fast, automatic response to a stimulus.

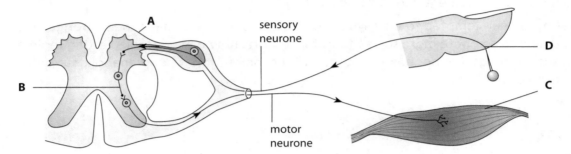

   (i) Name the parts labelled A and B. [2]

   (ii) Give the letter of the part that acts as the effector in the reflex action. [1]

   (iii) Describe **two** differences between a motor neurone and a sensory neurone. [2]

(b) Hormones are also involved in responding to stimuli.

   (i) Define the term *hormone*. [2]

   (ii) Copy and complete the table. [3]

Hormone	Gland that secretes it	Function of hormone
insulin		
		produces male secondary sexual characteristics
	adrenal gland	

(c) Plants also respond to stimuli. For example, a plant shoot grows towards light.

   (i) Give the correct term for the growth of a plant shoot towards light. [2]

   (ii) Suggest how this response helps the plant to survive. [2]

Supplement

2 **(a)** Auxin is a substance involved in the chemical control of plant growth. Auxin controls the response in which shoots grow towards the light.
Choose suitable words to complete these sentences.
Auxin is made in the .... of a shoot, from where it spreads through the plant. If light is shining from one side of the plant, the auxin .... on the .... side. Auxin makes the cells in this region ....
This makes the shoot grow towards the light. [4]

(b) The diagram shows a section through a human eye.

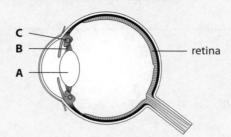

(i) Describe how parts **A**, **B** and **C** respond when the person focuses on an object that is close to the eye. [4]

(ii) The retina contains two types of receptor cells. Name these cells, and describe two differences between their functions. [3]

(c) People with type 1 diabetes have an increased risk of developing damage to cells in the retina, if they do not manage to control high blood glucose concentrations. Explain why someone with type 1 diabetes may have a high blood glucose concentration. [3]

3 **(a)** Alcohol and heroin are depressant drugs.

(i) Explain the meaning of the terms *drug* and *depressant*. [2]

(ii) People who drink large quantities of alcohol increase the risk of developing liver disease. Suggest why excessive alcohol consumption causes liver disease. [2]

(b) Nicotine is a drug that is contained in cigarette smoke.

(i) Outline the effects of nicotine on the body. [3]

(ii) Tar in cigarette smoke increases the risk of developing cancer. The graph shows the percentage of men and women who smoked and who developed lung cancer in a European country between 1972 and 2010.

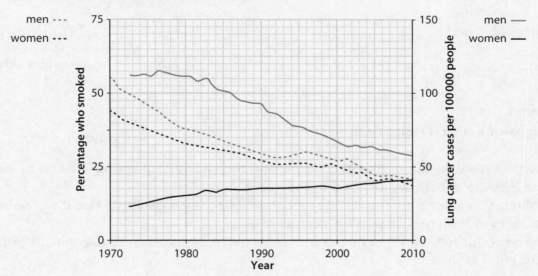

Compare the lung cancer rates in men and women between 1972 and 2010. [4]

(iii) Explain why these data alone do **not** provide firm evidence for a link between smoking and lung cancer. [4]

Asexual and sexual reproduction

Asexual reproduction involves:

- one parent only;
- the production of genetically identical offspring.

Sexual reproduction involves:

- either one or two parents;
- gametes (sex cells);
- fertilisation;
- the formation of a zygote;
- the production of genetically dissimilar offspring.

Definitions

Asexual reproduction – a process resulting in the production of genetically identical offspring from one parent.

Sexual reproduction – a process involving the fusion of the nuclei of two gametes (sex cells) to form a zygote and the production of offspring that are genetically different from each other.

Fertilisation – the fusion of gamete nuclei.

The diagrams show two examples of asexual reproduction.

The microscopic aquatic organism, *Hydra*, produces young by budding.

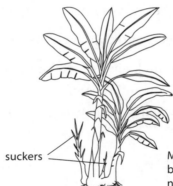

suckers

Many plants, such as this banana plant, produce new plants from suckers.

Supplement
Advantages of asexual reproduction

To a species in the wild

- If an organism is well-adapted to its environment, then all of its offspring will also be well-adapted, because they are genetically identical to their parent.
- Asexual reproduction requires only one parent, so when the organism is rare it will be able to reproduce even if there is no possible partner nearby.
- Asexual reproduction can often be faster than sexual reproduction, producing more young in a shorter period of time.

To people who grow crops

- The grower can produce large numbers of genetically identical plants, so that buyers know exactly what characteristics a plant will have.
- All the plants – for example a field of maize – will tend to grow to the same height and ripen at the same time, making harvesting and marketing easier.

Advantages of sexual reproduction

To a species in the wild

- If the environment changes – for example if the climate gets warmer, or if a new pathogen attacks the organisms – then there is a good chance that some of the genetically different offspring will have adaptations that allow them to survive. This enables evolution to take place.
- In flowering plants, sexual reproduction results in the production of seeds. These are dispersed far away from the parent plant, allowing colonisation of new areas, and reduction of competition between the new plants and the parent plant.

To people who grow crops

- Plant breeders can make use of the genetic variation that arises from sexual reproduction to breed new varieties of crops with different characteristics.

Fertilisation and zygotes

In sexual reproduction, two gametes join together. Their nuclei fuse to form a single nucleus. This is fertilisation.

Nuclei contain chromosomes. The normal cells of an organism contain two complete sets of chromosomes – two chromosomes of each kind. They are said to be **diploid** cells.

Gametes contain only one set of chromosomes – one chromosome of each kind. They are **haploid** cells.

When the nuclei of two gametes fuse together, they form a diploid **zygote**. The zygote then divides repeatedly to produce the hundreds of thousands of cells that make up a new organism.

haploid nucleus of male gamete

haploid nucleus of female gamete

diploid nucleus of zygote

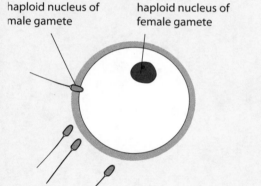
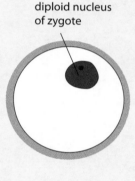

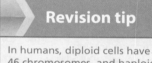

Revision tip

In humans, diploid cells have 46 chromosomes, and haploid cells (sperm and eggs) have 23 chromosomes. But other species have different numbers of chromosomes, so do not quote these numbers unless you are writing about humans.

Quick test

1. Describe **two** differences between asexual reproduction and sexual reproduction.
2. Give **two** examples of asexual reproduction.
3. What is a gamete?
4. What is fertilisation?

Supplement

5. Give **two** disadvantages of asexual reproduction.
6. Give **two** disadvantages of sexual reproduction.
7. The cells of a fruit fly have eight chromosomes. How many chromosomes are there in a gamete of a fruit fly?

Sexual reproduction in plants

The organs responsible for sexual reproduction in flowering plants are their flowers.

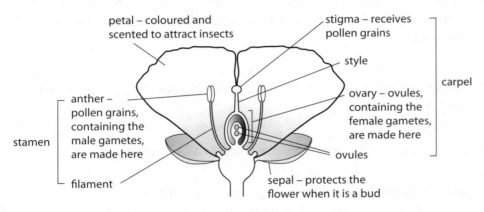

petal – coloured and scented to attract insects

stigma – receives pollen grains

style

carpel

anther – pollen grains, containing the male gametes, are made here

ovary – ovules, containing the female gametes, are made here

stamen

ovules

filament

sepal – protects the flower when it is a bud

Revision tip

Do not confuse the words 'plant' and 'flower'. A plant is the complete organism. A flower is a small part of a plant.

Insect-pollinated flowers have large petals to attract insects. They often produce sugary nectar, which insects come to feed on.

Wind-pollinated flowers have no need for large petals.

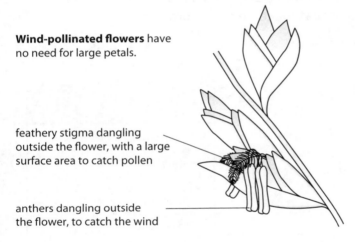

feathery stigma dangling outside the flower, with a large surface area to catch pollen

anthers dangling outside the flower, to catch the wind

Pollination

The male gametes of a flower are inside the pollen grains. The female gametes are inside the ovules. Pollen grains cannot move by themselves, so flowers rely on insects or the wind to carry pollen from the anther of one flower to the stigma of another.

Flowers that are insect-pollinated have pollen grains that are:

- often quite large and spiky, so that they can stick to the body of an insect;
- produced in relatively small quantities, because a lot of the pollen will be successfully transferred to another flower by an insect.

Flowers that are wind-pollinated have pollen grains that are:

- usually small and very light, so that they can easily be blown on the wind;
- produced in huge quantities, because only a tiny proportion of the pollen grains will land on a stigma.

Revision tip

It is wrong to say that pollen grains are the male gametes. The pollen grains **contain** the male gametes.

Fertilisation

Each pollen grain then grows a tube all the way from the stigma, down through the style, and into an ovule. A nucleus from the pollen grain travels down the tube. This male gamete nucleus then fuses with the female gamete nucleus inside the ovule. This produces a zygote.

The zygote grows into an embryo plant. The ovule grows into a seed, with the embryo plant inside it. Eventually, the seed grows into a new plant.

Supplement

Fertilisation happens when the nucleus of the male gamete fuses with the nucleus of the female gamete.

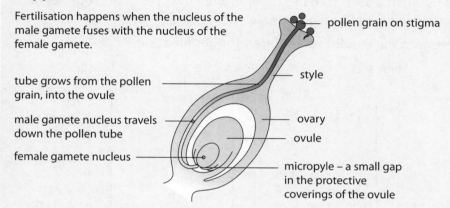

pollen grain on stigma

tube grows from the pollen grain, into the ovule

style

male gamete nucleus travels down the pollen tube

ovary

ovule

female gamete nucleus

micropyle – a small gap in the protective coverings of the ovule

Self-pollination and cross-pollination

Many plants produce both pollen and ovules. The same plant can therefore produce both male and female gametes.

Some flowers can pollinate their own stigmas with their own pollen. This is called **self-pollination**. When fertilisation takes place, their own male gametes fuse with their own female gametes.

Often, however, pollen is transferred from a flower on one plant to a flower on a different plant. This is called **cross-pollination**.

Both self-pollination and cross-pollination produce genetically different offspring. However, the differences are much greater when cross-pollination takes place. This is because in self-pollination all the alleles (forms) of the genes come from one parent, whereas in cross-pollination the two parents may have different alleles.

Advantages of self-pollination
- The plant does not have to rely on pollinators to transfer its pollen. Pollen can simply fall from the anther onto the stigma.
- If the plant is already well-adapted to its environment, then its offspring are also likely to be well-adapted.

Advantages of cross-pollination
- There is more genetic variation among the offspring, so there is a greater chance of at least some of them being able to survive if there are changes in the environment.

Seed germination

A seed contains an embryo plant. Seeds are covered by a tough testa, which protects the embryo plant inside. Seeds are usually quite dry when they leave the parent plant. They can often last for months or years before they germinate. This gives plenty of time for them to be dispersed far away from the parent.

Germination is the process that happens when a seed starts to grow into a new plant. All seeds need water, oxygen and a suitable temperature to make them germinate.

The diagram shows how you can investigate the conditions required for germination.

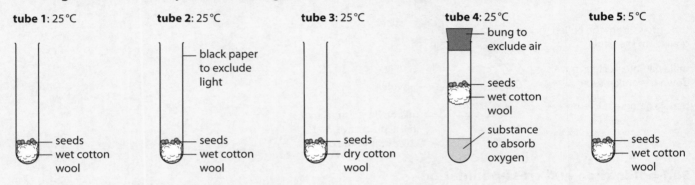

tube 1: 25 °C   **tube 2**: 25 °C   **tube 3**: 25 °C   **tube 4**: 25 °C   **tube 5**: 5 °C

tube 1: seeds / wet cotton wool

tube 2: black paper to exclude light / seeds / wet cotton wool

tube 3: seeds / dry cotton wool

tube 4: bung to exclude air / seeds / wet cotton wool / substance to absorb oxygen

tube 5: seeds / wet cotton wool

The seeds in tubes 1 and 2 will germinate. The seeds in tube 3 will not germinate, because they do not have water. The seeds in tube 4 will not germinate, because they do not have oxygen. The seeds in tube 5 will not germinate, because they are too cold. However, the seeds of some plants also need light for germination, so they will not germinate in tube 2.

Quick test

1. Name the part of a flower with each of these functions:

   (a) making the male gametes;

   (b) receiving pollen grains;

   (c) where fertilisation takes place.

2. Describe and explain **one** difference between the pollen of an insect-pollinated flower and a wind-pollinated flower.

3. Describe and explain **one** difference between the stigma of an insect-pollinated flower and a wind-pollinated flower.

4. List **three** conditions required for seed germination.

Supplement

5. Define *cross-pollination*.

6. State **one** advantage of self-pollination.

7. State **one** disadvantage of self-pollination.

8. Describe how a male gamete reaches a female gamete in a flower.

Sexual reproduction in humans

The diagrams show the structures and functions of the male and female reproductive organs.

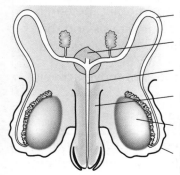

sperm duct: transfers sperm from testis to urethra

prostate gland: produces a fluid for sperm to swim in

urethra: carries sperm to the outside of the body

penis: inserts sperm into female's vagina

testis: sperm and the hormone testosterone are made here

scrotum: holds testes outside the body, where it is cooler for sperm production

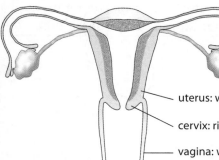

oviduct: transfers eggs from ovary; fertilisation takes place here

ovary: eggs and the hormones oestrogen and progesterone are made here

uterus: where the fetus develops

cervix: ring of muscle

vagina: where sperm are deposited, and through which the baby passes during birth

Fertilisation takes place in the oviducts.

- An egg cell is released from an ovary. This is called **ovulation**.
- During sexual intercourse, sperm cells are deposited at the top of the vagina.
- The sperm cells swim through the fluid covering the surfaces of the uterus and oviducts.
- The nucleus of one sperm cell fuses with the nucleus of the egg cell. This is fertilisation.
- This produces a zygote.

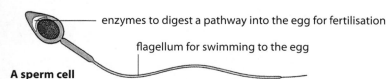

enzymes to digest a pathway into the egg for fertilisation

flagellum for swimming to the egg

A sperm cell

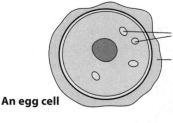

energy stores

jelly coat – changes after fertilisation to prevent any more sperm getting into the egg

An egg cell

Supplement

Adaptations of egg cells and sperm cells

The organelle in the head of a sperm that contains enzymes is called the **acrosome**.

Sperm cells contain a lot of mitochondria. Aerobic respiration in the mitochondria releases energy that is used to fuel the movement of the flagellum.

Human egg cells contain stores of glycogen and lipids. These provide energy for the zygote to allow it to divide repeatedly after fertilisation, forming an embryo.

The table compares human male gametes and female gametes.

Male gametes – sperm cells	Female gametes – egg cells
haploid nucleus with 23 chromosomes	haploid nucleus with 23 chromosomes
very small, to reduce the amount of energy needed for swimming	larger, to provide space for the stores of nutrients for the early embryo
has a tail and is motile (can move actively); sperm need to be able to swim to the egg	does not have a tail and is not motile; the egg is moved down the oviduct by peristalsis and the movement of cilia on cells lining the oviduct wall
has large numbers of mitochondria, for aerobic respiration to release energy for movement	has few mitochondria, as does not move actively
has an acrosome containing enzymes to help to penetrate the egg	does not have an acrosome
produced in huge numbers; sperm are very small, so making large numbers of them does not use too much energy	produced in small numbers; eggs are relatively large, so making lots of them would waste a lot of energy; also, it is best if only one or two eggs are fertilised at the same time, so that only one or two embryos develop in the mother's uterus at the same time

Development of the fetus

The cell produced when a sperm cell fertilises an egg cell is called a **zygote**.

The zygote divides repeatedly to form a little ball of cells called an **embryo**.

The embryo moves down the oviduct into the uterus. Here, it sinks into the soft lining. This is called **implantation**.

The embryo gradually develops into a **fetus**. A **placenta** grows in the wall of the uterus, connected to the fetus by the **umbilical cord**. The placenta is where substances are exchanged between the blood of the mother and the blood of the fetus. The umbilical cord transports substances between the fetus and the placenta.

The fetus is surrounded by an **amniotic sac**. This makes a fluid called **amniotic fluid**. This helps to support the fetus as it grows, and protects it from mechanical shocks.

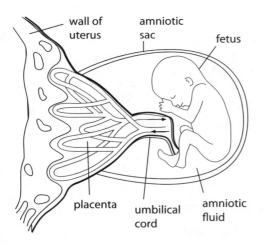

For the first 11 weeks of pregnancy, the fetus gradually develops a more complex structure. All the different organs are formed. For the rest of the pregnancy, the fetus grows steadily bigger. By nine months, it is ready to be born.

Functions of the placenta

The placenta is the organ where exchange of materials between the mother's blood and the blood of the developing fetus takes place.

The blood of the mother and the blood of the fetus do **not** mix. They flow close together inside the placenta, but are kept separate from one another.

Oxygen, water and dissolved nutrients (such as amino acids and glucose) diffuse from the mother's blood into the fetus's blood.

Urea and carbon dioxide diffuse from the fetus's blood into the mother's blood.

Most toxins and pathogens cannot pass through the placenta from the mother into the fetus's blood. However, some toxins can get through. These include:

- nicotine and carbon monoxide from cigarette smoke;
- alcohol;
- some viruses, for example the rubella virus.

Function of the umbilical cord

The fetus's blood flows to the placenta through an artery in the umbilical cord. It flows back to the fetus through two veins in the umbilical cord.

Ante-natal care, labour and birth

Ante-natal means 'before birth'.

A pregnant woman should try to take care of her own health and the health of her growing fetus. This involves:

- Eating well. She will need to eat a little more of everything, to supply her fetus's needs as well as her own. In particular, she will need more iron to form her baby's blood, more calcium to form her baby's bones and teeth, and more protein for her baby's growth.
- Not smoking. Nicotine and carbon monoxide from cigarette smoke will go into her baby's blood. They can slow down its growth so that it is born less healthy and smaller than it would otherwise be.
- Not drinking alcohol. While small amounts of alcohol seem to do no harm, babies born to mothers who drink heavily may have less well-developed brains.

Labour is the process of giving birth.

- The strong muscles of the uterus wall begin to contract and relax. At first, the contractions are relatively gentle, with quite long time intervals between them. They gradually get stronger and more frequent.
- The muscle contractions dilate (widen) the cervix, so that the baby's head can pass through.
- The muscle contractions may cause the amniotic sac to break, so that the amniotic fluid passes out through the vagina. However, this often doesn't happen until a later stage of the birth.
- The muscle contractions push the baby through the cervix and vagina.
- After the baby has been delivered, it is still attached to the placenta by the umbilical cord. A nurse or midwife will cut the cord – it contains no nerves, so this is painless. The cord is clamped or tied.
- The placenta then breaks away from the wall of the uterus and passes out through the vagina. It is called the afterbirth.

Supplement

Breast-feeding and bottle-feeding

Like all mammals, human mothers produce milk in mammary glands. Many mothers choose to breast-feed their baby. The advantages of this are:

- Breast milk is free.
- Breast milk contains antibodies that help to protect the baby from pathogens, until its own immune system has fully developed.
- Breast milk is at the perfect temperature.
- Breast milk contains exactly the right combination of nutrients for the baby.
- The composition of breast milk changes as the baby grows, so that it gets an ideal diet at each stage of development.

Disadvantages include:

- Mothers sometimes have difficulty in breast-feeding, so that their baby does not get enough milk, or the mother finds it very stressful. Bottle-feeding solves both of these problems.
- If a mother is HIV positive, breast-feeding runs a risk of passing on the virus to her baby, especially if she is not receiving treatment with antiretroviral drugs.

Other mothers choose to use formula milk. The advantages of this are:

- Bottle-feeding allows the father or another person to take over some of the work of feeding the baby. This can allow the mother to get more sleep, or to work if she needs or wants to do so.
- Bottle-feeding means that the baby gets good quality milk, even if the mother is unwell or malnourished.

The disadvantages of this are:

- Formula milk is expensive to buy.
- If it is not carefully prepared, formula milk can become contaminated with bacteria that could make the baby ill.
- Formula milk does not contain antibodies.

Sex hormones

The testes produce the hormone **testosterone**. The functions of testosterone include:

- stimulating sperm production;
- causing development of male secondary sexual characteristics during puberty, such as deepening of the voice and broadening of the shoulders.

The ovaries produce **oestrogen**. The functions of oestrogen include:

- helping to control the menstrual cycle (see below);
- causing development of female secondary sexual characteristics during puberty, such as development of breasts and widening of the hips.

The menstrual cycle

After puberty, until the age of about 50, a monthly sequence of changes takes place in a woman's reproductive system.

Development of a corpus luteum
In the ovary, the space where the egg came from develops into a corpus luteum. The lining of the uterus remains thick, in case the egg is fertilised.

Menstruation
If an egg is not fertilised, the lining of the uterus breaks down and is lost through the vagina.

Ovulation
An egg is released from one of the ovaries. The lining of the uterus continues to develop, in case the egg is fertilised.

Repair
The lining of the uterus gradually builds up again. In the ovaries, an egg develops.

Supplement

Hormones in the menstrual cycle

The graph shows the times of the menstrual cycle when oestrogen, progesterone, follicle stimulating hormone (FSH) and luteinising hormone (LH) are produced. The table shows the sites of their production, and their functions.

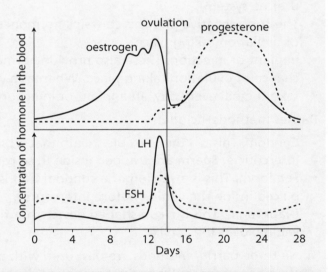

Hormone	Site of production	When secreted	Function
oestrogen	follicle in the ovary	all the time, but more during the middle of the menstrual cycle	stimulates the lining of the uterus to grow thicker
progesterone	corpus luteum in the ovary	during the second half of the menstrual cycle	maintains the thick lining of the uterus
	placenta during pregnancy	throughout pregnancy	
FSH	pituitary gland	mostly during the first half of the menstrual cycle	causes a follicle to develop and produce an egg
LH	pituitary gland	in the first half of the menstrual cycle, with a surge just before ovulation	causes ovulation – the release of an egg from the ovary

Birth control

Birth control means preventing pregnancy when this is not required, and increasing the chances of getting pregnant when this is desired.

Methods of reducing the risk of becoming pregnant

Natural methods include:

- Abstinence. This means not having sexual intercourse.
- Monitoring the menstrual cycle. A woman's body temperature usually rises very slightly just before ovulation, and the mucus in the vagina becomes slightly more liquid. She should avoid intercourse at this time and for about a week afterwards, as there is likely to be an egg in the oviduct that could be fertilised.

Chemical methods include:

- Using an IUD (intra-uterine device). This is a loop or coil of plastic or copper that is placed inside the uterus by a doctor. It reduces the chances of sperm swimming through the uterus to the oviducts. A similar device, but which also releases hormones that reduce even more the chances of sperm reaching the oviducts, is called an IUS (intra-uterine system).
- The contraceptive pill. This contains hormones that reduce the chance of ovulation taking place.
- Implant or injection. These also provide hormones that reduce the chance of ovulation taking place. Whereas a woman must remember to take the pill every day, an implant or injection lasts for a long time.

Barrier methods include:

- Condom. This is a thin, flexible sheath that is placed over the penis before intercourse. Sperm are trapped inside it, so cannot enter the vagina.
- Femidom. This is a version of a condom that is used by women. It is placed inside the vagina before intercourse.
- Diaphragm. This is a cup-shaped device that fits inside a woman's vagina, over the cervix.

These three barrier methods are best used with a spermicidal cream, which kills any sperm that might manage to find a way around the barrier.

Surgical methods include:

- Vasectomy. A man's sperm ducts are cut and tied off, so that sperm cannot pass from the testes to the penis.
- Female sterilisation. A woman's oviducts are cut and tied off, so that eggs cannot be reached by sperm.

Supplement

The contraceptive pill contains oestrogen and progesterone. These inhibit the production of FSH, which stops follicles and eggs developing in the woman's ovaries.

Fertility treatments

Some couples who want to have children are not able to do so. There are several kinds of treatment that may be able to help them.

Fertility drugs These are hormones that can be given to a woman whose menstrual cycle is not working properly, or who is not producing eggs. She may be given FSH to encourage follicles to develop, and LH to stimulate ovulation.

Artificial insemination is used when there is a problem with the man's sperm. Semen (a mixture of sperm in fluid) can be inserted into the woman's vagina and allowed to fertilise the egg in the normal way.

In vitro **fertilisation** IVF is used when there are problems with either the man's or the woman's reproductive systems. Eggs are collected from the woman, and placed in a dish in a laboratory. Sperm are collected from the man, and added to the eggs. If all goes well, some of the sperm will fertilise the eggs. The zygotes divide to form tiny embryos. One or more embryos are then inserted into the woman's uterus and allowed to implant. With luck, at least one of these will develop into a fetus and be born in the usual way.

To prepare for IVF, the woman will be given FSH and sometimes also LH to help her to produce more eggs than usual in her ovaries. These drugs will be given before the eggs are collected. After this has been done, she may be given progesterone to make sure that the lining of her uterus is ready to receive the embryos.

There are many possible **social implications** of fertility treatment.

Positive implications
- It can relieve stress that some couples experience because they cannot have children.
- In a country with a falling population, it can increase the number of births.

Negative implications
- The use of fertility treatment may conflict with religious beliefs.
- There is an increased risk of multiple births, which can place stress on a family.
- The treatment is expensive, so only some couples may be able to afford it.

Sexually transmitted infections

STIs are infections caused by pathogens that pass from one person to another through sexual contact.

Definition
Sexually transmitted infection – an infection that is transmitted via body fluids through sexual contact.

The **human immunodeficiency virus**, **HIV**, is an STI. It can be transmitted:

- through sexual intercourse, when it is passed from one person to another in fluids in the penis or vagina;
- through blood-to-blood contact, for example in a blood transfusion or by sharing needles for injections;
- through breast milk, from mother to baby.

The spread of HIV can be controlled by:

- educating people about its methods of spreading, so that each person can reduce their risk of infection through their behaviour;
- testing people for HIV, so that a person who has the virus knows that they are HIV positive and can avoid passing the virus to anyone else;
- using condoms during sexual intercourse;
- not reusing needles that have been used for injection;
- treating pregnant women with HIV with antiretroviral drugs, which reduces the chance of passing the virus to the fetus or newborn baby.

This virus causes the disease AIDS (acquired immune deficiency syndrome), in which the immune system stops working properly. A person with AIDS is at risk of serious infections, which are likely eventually to kill them. However, treatment with antiretroviral drugs can keep the virus under control, so that the person can continue to lead an almost normal life for a long time.

Supplement

HIV attacks the immune system. The viruses invade a group of lymphocytes (white blood cells) called T cells. The viruses multiply inside the T cells, eventually destroying the cells. T cells are important in killing viruses inside the body, and also in destroying cancer cells. T cells also help other lymphocytes to produce antibodies against viruses and other pathogens.

It may take many years after infection with HIV for large numbers of T cells to be destroyed. Once this happens, the person is said to have AIDS. The loss of T cells and reduced ability to make antibodies means that they lose their protection against pathogens, and also have an increased risk of developing several kinds of cancer.

Quick test

1. State the function of the prostate gland.
2. Define *fertilisation*.
3. State **two** ways in which the structure of a sperm cell differs from that of an egg cell.
4. In which part of the female body does fertilisation take place?
5. Write these processes in the correct order:
   implantation   ovulation   fertilisation
6. Explain the difference between a zygote and an embryo.
7. Give **two** functions of oestrogen.
8. Describe a barrier method of birth control.
9. Give one example of a sexually transmitted infection.
10. State **two** ways of reducing the spread of this sexually transmitted infection.

Supplement

11. Describe the function of the acrosome in a sperm cell.
12. Name **two** substances that pass from a fetus's blood to its mother's blood, in the placenta.
13. Name **one** toxin that can cross the placenta to the fetus.
14. Name the sites of production of
    (a) oestrogen;
    (b) FSH.
15. Name **two** places where progesterone is secreted.
16. State the function of progesterone.
17. Explain the difference between artificial insemination and *in vitro* fertilisation.

Exam-style practice questions

1 **(a)** AIDS is a disease caused by the human immunodeficiency virus, HIV. AIDS is a sexually transmitted infection. Define the term *sexually transmitted infection* (STI). [2]

(b) The graph shows the number of pregnant women in developing countries who were living with HIV, between 2000 and 2014. It also shows the number of these women who were receiving treatment with antiretroviral drugs (ARVs).

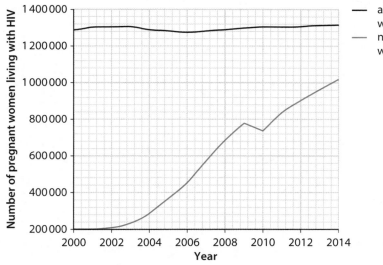

(i) Describe the changes in the number of pregnant women receiving ARVs between 2000 and 2014. [3]

(ii) Describe the changes in the proportion of pregnant women living with HIV who received ARVs between 2000 and 2014. [2]

(iii) Treatment with ARVs reduces the risk of a pregnant woman with HIV passing the virus to her child. Suggest **one** reason why not all pregnant women with HIV receive treatment with ARVs. [1]

(c) State **one** way, other than from a mother to her child, that HIV is transmitted. [1]

(d) State **one** method of birth control that also helps to reduce the transmission of HIV. [1]

Supplement

2 **(a)** The diagram shows a sperm cell.

(i) In humans, the diploid number of chromosomes is 46. State the number of chromosomes in the nucleus of a sperm cell. [1]

(ii) Describe the function of part **A**. [2]

(iii) Explain how parts **B** and **C** adapt the sperm cell for its function. [3]

(b) Artificial insemination, AI, is often used when breeding farm animals, such as horses.

   (i) Outline how artificial insemination is carried out. [3]

   (ii) Semen collected for AI can be frozen, allowing it to be stored for a long time, or transported over long distances. The graph shows the motility of sperm from frozen horse semen that is untreated, or treated with a drug called pentoxifyline, for the first 150 minutes after thawing.

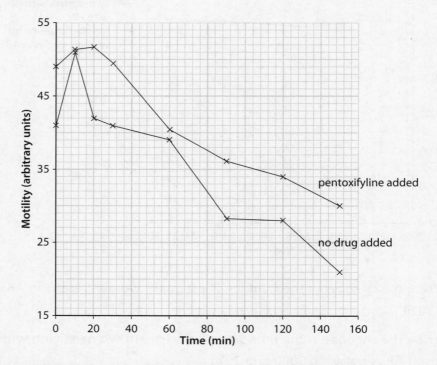

Describe how the motility of untreated semen changes over time. [3]

   (iii) With reference to the data in the graph, explain how treating thawed semen with pentoxifyline could increase the success rate of AI. [4]

3 **(a)** The diagram shows a pollen grain on the stigma of a flower.

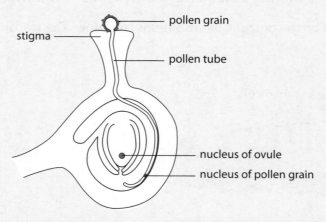

   (i) State **one** feature, visible on the diagram, that suggests that the flower is pollinated by insects. [1]

(ii) Which structure, labelled on the diagram, is the male gamete? [1]

(iii) With reference to the structures labelled on the diagram, describe how fertilisation will take place. [3]

(b) (i) Explain the difference between self-pollination and cross-pollination. [3]

(ii) Many flowers are adapted to prevent self-pollination. Explain the advantage of preventing self-pollination. [2]

(c) Bumble-bees are important pollinators of fruit crops. There is concern that the use of pesticides based on nicotine, called neonicotinoids, may reduce the effectiveness of pollination by bumble-bees.

Researchers divided an area of flowering apple trees into three groups.

- In one group, no pesticide was used.
- In the second group, the trees were sprayed with 2.4 ppb (parts per billion) of neonicotinoid.
- In the third group, the trees were sprayed with 10 ppb of neonicotinoid.

The researchers measured the number of bumble-bees visiting the apple flowers per minute. Several months later, they also counted the number of seeds that developed in each apple. The results are shown in the table.

Treatment of trees	No pesticide	2.4 ppb neonicotinoid	10 ppb neonicotinoid
mean number of bumble-bees visiting flowers in one minute	0.08	0.05	0.04
mean number of seeds per apple fruit	4.68	5.20	3.00

(i) With reference to the data in the table, describe the effect of neonicotinoids on the activity of bumble-bees. [2]

(ii) Explain why the researchers waited several months before counting the number of seeds in each apple. [1]

(iii) Suggest an explanation for the effect of neonicotinoids on the mean number of seeds per apple fruit. [3]

Genes and chromosomes

The nucleus of every cell contains **chromosomes**. Each chromosome is a long thread of a chemical called **DNA**.

DNA carries information that is passed on from parents to offspring, in the nuclei of the male and female gametes. Passing on DNA from one generation to the next is called **inheritance**.

Each thread of DNA is made up of many **genes**. Each gene contains information for making a particular protein.

Definitions

Inheritance – the transmission of genetic information from generation to generation.
Chromosome – a thread-like structure made of DNA, which carries genetic information in the form of genes.
Gene – a length of DNA that codes for a protein.

Supplement

DNA

The information carried in DNA is in the form of a code. This is known as the genetic code.

Each DNA molecule contains tens of thousands of smaller molecules called **bases**. The code is made up of four bases, called **A**, **C**, **T** and **G**. The sequence in which these bases are arranged in the DNA determines which proteins will be made in the cell.

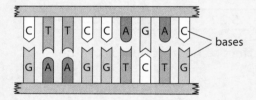
bases

Proteins are made of amino acids. The sequence of amino acids in a protein determines the structure, and therefore the function, of that protein.

So the sequence of bases in a DNA molecule determines the sequence of amino acids in the proteins that are made in the cell. This in turn affects the **functions** of the proteins. You will remember that proteins have many different functions, including enzymes, antibodies and receptors for neurotransmitters. So the proteins that are made in a cell determine the features of that cell, and of the organism of which it is part.

Revision tip

Do not confuse bases and amino acids. DNA is made up of a sequence of bases. Proteins are made up of a sequence of amino acids.

RNA and protein synthesis

DNA is in the nucleus. Protein synthesis happens on ribosomes in the cytoplasm. Because DNA contains all the information about how the cell and organism will develop, it is too precious to be allowed out of the nucleus. Instead, a copy of this information – the base sequence – is made by another molecule, called **messenger RNA**. This is called **mRNA** for short.

- In the nucleus, a molecule of mRNA is made, copying the sequence of bases of one gene on the DNA.
- The mRNA travels out of the nucleus into the cytoplasm.

- The mRNA goes to a ribosome.
- The ribosome has a groove in it, through which the mRNA moves. As each little group of bases in the sequence lies in this groove, amino acids are brought to the ribosome. The ribosome follows the sequence of bases in the mRNA to link together amino acids in the correct sequence to make a protein.

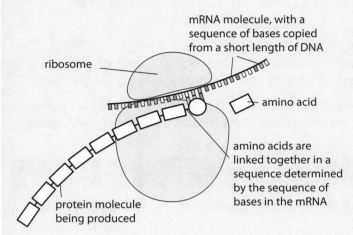

mRNA molecule, with a sequence of bases copied from a short length of DNA

ribosome

amino acid

amino acids are linked together in a sequence determined by the sequence of bases in the mRNA

protein molecule being produced

Gene expression

All the cells in your body contain exactly the same genes. However, in each cell only some of these genes are used to make proteins.

For example, the cells in your scalp use information in some genes that code for making keratin, the protein in hair. The cells in your heart contain exactly these same genes, but the cells do not use their information, and do not make keratin.

When a cell uses the instructions on a gene to make a protein, we say that the gene is **expressed**. Each cell only expresses the genes for the proteins that it needs, to enable it to carry out its specific functions.

Chromosomes, genes and alleles

In human cells, there are 46 chromosomes. Each chromosome is a long strand of DNA, and is made up of many genes.

In human cells, these chromosomes are made up of 23 pairs. They are numbered 1 to 23. Each pair of chromosomes has the same genes in the same places. For example, our two chromosome 4s both have a gene for hair colour on them. So we have two copies of this hair colour gene in each of our cells.

The copies of this gene for hair colour can come in different varieties. For example, one of them might carry instructions for producing red hair, and another might carry instructions for producing brown hair.

Different varieties of the same gene are called **alleles**.

Definition
Allele – a version of a gene.

Haploid and diploid cells

Almost all the cells in our bodies contain two complete sets of chromosomes in their nuclei. They are said to be diploid cells.

Gametes – egg cells and sperm cells – contain only one set of chromosomes. They are said to be haploid cells.

When an egg cell and a sperm cell fuse together, the single set of chromosomes from the mother joins with the single set of chromosomes from the father. So each zygote has two copies of each chromosome – a maternal chromosome from the mother, and a paternal chromosome from the father.

The zygote divides repeatedly by mitosis, copying each chromosome perfectly every time. This means that normal body cells have two copies of every chromosome, and therefore two copies of every gene. Gametes have only one copy of every gene.

Definitions
Haploid nucleus – a nucleus containing a single set of unpaired chromosomes, for example in gametes.   **Diploid nucleus** – a nucleus containing two sets of chromosomes, for example in body cells.

Quick test

1. Define the term *gene*.
2. Which part of your body cells contains DNA?
3. How is DNA from a parent passed to their children?
4. What is the meaning of the word *allele*?

Supplement

5. Each molecule of DNA is made up of a sequence of bases. How many different kinds of bases are there?
6. Where in a cell does protein synthesis take place?
7. What determines the sequence of amino acids that are linked together to make a particular protein?
8. Explain why the sequence of amino acids in a protein is important.
9. Name the molecule that carries information from DNA to the site of protein synthesis.
10. How many copies of each gene does an animal have in: (a) a cell in its skin; (b) an egg cell?

Cell division

When a cell divides, it is very important all the information contained in its DNA is copied and passed on to the new cells (daughter cells).

There are two kinds of cell division:

- Mitosis is used to make new cells that are exactly like the parent cell. When the nucleus divides, a copy of each chromosome is passed on to the nucleus of each daughter cell. The new cells are genetically identical to their parent cell and to each other.
- Meiosis is used to make gametes. Only half of the chromosomes from the parent cell are passed on to the nucleus of each daughter cell. The daughter cells are genetically different from their parent cell and from each other.

Definitions

Mitosis – nuclear division giving rise to cells that are genetically identical.
Meiosis – nuclear division giving rise to cells that are genetically different.

Revision tip

You must take care spelling mitosis and meiosis. Practise them until you get it right every time. Make sure your writing is really clear, so that an examiner cannot mistake your meaning.

Mitosis is used for:

- making new cells for growth;
- making new cells to repair damaged tissues or to replace worn-out cells;
- making new cells to produce a new organism by asexual reproduction.

Meiosis is used for making gametes.

Supplement

If you are studying the extension syllabus, you need to learn a more detailed definition of meiosis.

Definition

Meiosis – reduction division in which the chromosome number is halved from diploid to haploid resulting in genetically different cells.

Meiosis produces daughter cells that are genetically different from the parent cell in two ways:

- They have only half the number of chromosomes.
- They contain different combinations of maternal and paternal chromosomes.

The diagrams summarise some of the events in mitosis and meiosis. For simplicity, only one pair of chromosomes is shown.

Mitosis

1 The nucleus of this cell contains one pair of chromosomes.

2 Just before mitosis begins, each chromosome is copied exactly. This means that the sequence of bases on the DNA molecule in the chromosome is copied perfectly, making another DNA molecule with exactly the same sequence of bases.

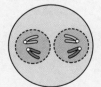

3 During mitosis, the two copies of each chromosome split apart.

4 When mitosis is complete, two daughter nuclei are formed, each with two chromosomes exactly like the nucleus of the original parent cell.

Meiosis

1 The nucleus of this cell contains one pair of chromosomes.

2 Just as in meiosis, a perfect copy is made of each chromosome.

3 The two chromosomes pair up.

4 The two chromosomes in the pair separate from one another.

5 Each daughter cell has only one chromosome in its nucleus, instead of two. The number of chromosomes has been halved. Haploid cells have been made from a diploid cell.

6 Each daughter cell then divides again, just like mitosis. So four haploid daughter cells are eventually formed from one diploid parent cell.

After a daughter cell has been formed, it may become **specialised** for a particular function. In humans, for example, a cell might become a blood cell, a muscle cell or a rod cell. It will do this by expressing the particular genes that are needed to make this particular kind of cell. Usually, once a cell has become specialised, it keeps this same function to the end of its life.

Some cells do not become specialised. They retain the ability to turn into different kinds of cells. These unspecialised cells are called **stem cells**. They can divide by mitosis to produce daughter cells that can become specialised for different functions.

Mitosis	Meiosis
produces two genetically identical daughter cells	produces four genetically different daughter cells
can be carried out by haploid cells or diploid cells	can only be carried out by diploid cells
used for growth, repair and asexual reproduction	used for making gametes

Quick test

1. Name the two types of cell division.
2. Which type of cell division is used for growth?
3. Which type of cell division is used for making gametes?

Supplement

4. A cell contains eight chromosomes. How many chromosomes will its daughter cells contain after it has divided by mitosis?
5. How many chromosomes will its daughter cells contain if it divides by meiosis?
6. What is a stem cell?

We have seen that every cell, except gametes, contains two copies of each chromosome. They therefore have two copies of each gene.

There are different varieties of most genes. These varieties are called **alleles**.

We can use letters to represent alleles. We use the same letter for the same gene, with a capital letter to represent one allele and a small letter for a different allele.

For example, imagine that an animal can have brown fur or white fur. Each cell in each animal has two copies of the fur colour gene. There are two different alleles of the fur colour gene. Allele **A** gives brown fur and allele **a** gives white fur.

There are three possible combinations of these alleles that the animal can have in its cells – **AA**, **Aa** or **aa**. The combination of alleles in the cell is called the **genotype** of the organism.

If both the alleles are the same, the genotype is **homozygous**.

If the two alleles are different, the genotype is **heterozygous**.

Often, one allele is **dominant** and the other **recessive**. A dominant allele always has an effect on the organism. A recessive allele only has an effect if there is no dominant allele present. Normally, the dominant allele is represented by a capital letter and the recessive allele by a small letter.

This means that an organism with the genotype **AA** or **Aa** has brown fur. Only an organism with the genotype **aa** has white fur.

The features of the organism are its **phenotype**.

Genotype	Phenotype
AA	brown fur
Aa	brown fur
aa	white fur

Definitions

Genotype – the genetic make-up of an organism in terms of the alleles present.
Phenotype – the observable features of an organism.
Homozygous – having two identical alleles of a particular gene.
Heterozygous – having two different alleles of a particular gene.
Dominant – an allele that is expressed if it is present.
Recessive – an allele that is only expressed when there is no dominant allele of the gene present.

Revision tip

Remember that you need to learn every definition carefully. You will find this much easier if you make sure that you *understand* them first.

Genetic diagrams

A genetic diagram is a way of showing how alleles are passed on from parents to their offspring.

We can use a cross between a heterozygous brown animal and a white one as an example.

- First, show the phenotypes and genotypes of the parents. The brown animal is heterozygous, so its genotype must be **Aa**. The white animal must be homozygous, **aa**.

Parental phenotypes	brown	white
Parental genotypes	**Aa**	**aa**

- Next, show the genotypes of the gametes that each parent can make. Remember that gametes contain only one of each kind of gene, so they will only have one allele.
  The heterozygous brown parent can make two kinds of gametes. Half of them will have an **A** allele, and the other half will have an **a** allele. The white parent can only make one kind of gamete. All their gametes will have an **a** allele.
  By convention, we draw a circle around the gamete genotypes.

Gamete genotypes

- Next, show the different possible genotypes of the cells that will be formed when these gametes fuse together. You can see that either an A gamete or an a gamete from the brown parent can fuse with an a gamete from the white parent. Drawing a table is a good way of showing this.

Offspring genotypes and phenotypes

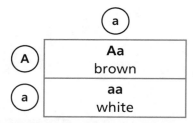

- Finally, summarise what you have discovered about the genotypes and phenotypes of the offspring. Here, we have shown that the offspring from these parents can be either brown or white. We can see that there is an equal chance of getting brown or white offspring. In other words, we would expect the ratio of brown : white offspring to be 1 : 1.

Here is what we would expect to happen if the parents were both heterozygous.

Parental phenotypes	brown	brown
Parental genotypes	**Aa**	**Aa**
Gametes	(A) and (a)	(A) and (a)

Offspring genotypes and phenotypes

	(A)	(a)
(A)	AA brown	Aa brown
(a)	Aa brown	aa white

Summary: We would expect a ratio of approximately 3 brown : 1 white.

Pure-breeding

If an organism is said to be **pure-breeding**, it means that if it is bred with another organism like itself, all the offspring will look the same as the parents. For example, in the example above, if you breed two pure-breeding brown organisms together, all the offspring will be brown.

Pure-breeding individuals must therefore be homozygous. A pure-breeding brown organism has the genotype **AA**.

Heterozygous organisms are not pure-breeding. We have seen that if you breed two heterozygous brown organisms together, some of their offspring will have the genotype aa and be white.

Pedigree diagrams

A pedigree diagram is a chart that shows the phenotypes of individuals in a family over several generations.

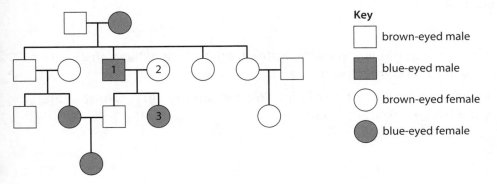

Key

☐ brown-eyed male

◼ blue-eyed male

◯ brown-eyed female

● blue-eyed female

Sex inheritance

In humans, the 23rd pair of chromosomes are the sex chromosomes. In women, there are two X chromosomes. In men, there is one X chromosome and one much shorter Y chromosome.

We can show how sex is inherited using a genetic diagram.

Parental phenotypes	male	female
Parental genotypes	**XY**	**XX**
Gametes	ⓧ and ⓨ	ⓧ

Offspring genotypes and phenotypes

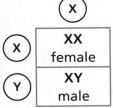

	ⓧ
ⓧ	**XX** female
ⓨ	**XY** male

Summary: We would expect a ratio of approximately 1 male : 1 female.

Supplement

Test crosses

In the example of the organisms with brown or white fur, we have seen that a brown organism can have the genotype **AA** or **Aa**. We can find out which genotype it has by crossing it with an organism with white fur, which must have the genotype **aa**.

If any of the offspring have white fur, then the brown parent must have an allele for white fur, so its genotype must be **Aa**.

If none of the offspring have white fur, then it is probable that the brown parent did not have an allele for white fur, so its genotype is probably **AA**.

Co-dominance

Sometimes, two alleles may be neither dominant nor recessive. Instead, both of them have an effect on a heterozygous organism. They are said to be co-dominant.

For example, in some plants the flowers can be red, white or pink. We can use the letter C to stand for the gene for flower colour. The two alleles are written C^R and C^W.

Genotype	Phenotype
$C^R C^R$	red flowers
$C^R C^W$	pink flowers
$C^W C^W$	white flowers

Human blood groups are an example of co-dominance. Here, there are three different alleles – I^A, I^B, and I^o.

Genotype	Phenotype
$I^A I^A$	blood group A
$I^A I^B$	blood group AB
$I^A I^o$	blood group A
$I^B I^B$	blood group B
$I^B I^o$	blood group B
$I^o I^o$	blood group O

Alleles I^A and I^B are co-dominant. Both of them are dominant to allele I^o, which is recessive.

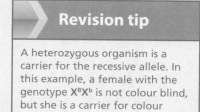

Revision tip

Whenever you have a genetics question to answer, it is always a good idea to start by drawing up a table like this one, showing all the possible genotypes and phenotypes. It will make answering the question much faster, and you are less likely to make mistakes.

Sex linkage

Some genes are carried on the X chromosome. This means that a woman has two copies (one on each X chromosome), but a man only has one copy of these genes. These genes are said to be **sex-linked**.

One example is a gene that determines colour vision. We can use the symbol **B** for the normal allele, and **b** for a faulty allele that causes colour blindness. **B** is dominant and **b** is recessive.

When we write a person's genotypes for a sex-linked gene, we have to write the X and Y as well as the symbol for the allele, like this:

Genotype	Phenotype
$X^B X^B$	female with normal vision
$X^B X^b$	female with normal vision
$X^b X^b$	colour-blind female
$X^B Y$	male with normal vision
$X^b Y$	colour-blind male

Revision tip

A heterozygous organism is a carrier for the recessive allele. In this example, a female with the genotype $X^B X^b$ is not colour blind, but she is a carrier for colour blindness.

We can use genetic diagrams to show how this sex-linked gene is inherited.

Parental phenotypes	normal female	normal male
Parental genotypes	$X^B X^b$	$X^B Y$

Gametes X^B and X^b X^B and Y

Offspring genotypes and phenotypes

	X^B	Y
X^B	$X^B X^B$ normal female	$X^B Y$ normal male
X^b	$X^B X^b$ normal female	$X^b Y$ colour-blind male

Summary: We would expect a ratio of 2 normal females : 1 normal male : 1 colour-blind male.

Definition

Sex-linked characteristic – a characteristic in which the gene responsible is located on a sex chromosome and that this makes it more common in one sex than in the other.

Quick test

1. A plant has two alleles for the gene for leaf shape. Allele **P** is dominant and gives smooth leaves. Allele **p** is recessive and gives spiky leaves. Construct a table to show the three possible genotypes and their corresponding phenotypes.

2. One of these plants is pure-breeding for smooth leaves. What is its genotype?

3. An organism has the genotype **Gg**. What are the genotypes of its gametes?

4. Look at the pedigree diagram on page 103. Use the symbols **B** for the allele for brown eyes and **b** for the allele for blue eyes. **B** is dominant and **b** is recessive.

   (a) What is the phenotype of person 3?

   (b) What is the genotype of person 3?

   (c) What is the genotype of person 1?

   (d) Work out the genotype of person 2.

5. Construct a complete genetic diagram to show the possible genotypes and phenotypes of the children born to a blue-eyed man and a heterozygous brown-eyed woman.

Supplement

6. What is the term for a genetic cross in which a heterozygous organism is bred with a homozygous recessive one?

7. A man with blood group A and a woman with blood group B have a child with blood group O. Construct a genetic diagram to explain how this is possible.

8. Haemophilia is a sex-linked characteristic. It is caused by a recessive allele, h, which is found on the X chromosome.

   (a) Write down the genotype of a man with haemophilia.

   (b) Explain why a man with haemophilia cannot pass on this condition to his son.

Variation and selection

Living organisms belonging to the same species look similar to one another. However, two individuals are never completely identical. They show **variation**.

> **Definition**
>
> <u>Variation</u> – differences between individuals of the same species.

Individuals are different because:

- they have different combinations of alleles of their **genes**
- they experience different **environments**.

Genotypic and phenotypic variation

We have seen how organisms with different genotypes can have different phenotypes. However, this is not always the case if one allele is dominant and another is recessive. An organism with the genotype **Bb** may have brown fur, exactly the same colour as an organism with **BB**. So genotypic variation does not always result in phenotypic variation.

Also, two organisms with the same genotype may not have the same phenotype, if their environments are different. Two people with the same genotype for height may grow to different heights if they have different diets as they grow up.

Continuous and discontinuous variation

Human height is an example of **continuous variation**. A person may be any height between the very smallest and the very tallest. There are no distinct categories. The table and histogram show some results from measuring the height of 25 children in a class.

Tongue rolling is an example of **discontinuous variation**. A person either can roll their tongue or they cannot. There are two distinct categories, with no intermediates. The bar chart shows how many children could roll their tongues.

> **Revision tip**
>
> Stating that height is an example of continuous variation doesn't mean it is something that varies during your life, that is, getting taller. It means that, in a population, a person can be any height.

Height (cm)	145–149	150–154	155–159	160–164	165–169	170–174
Number of people	2	2	5	8	6	2

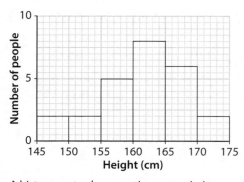

A histogram to show continuous variation.

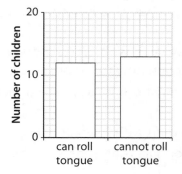

A bar chart to show discontinuous variation.

> **Revision tip**
>
> When there are distinct categories on the x-axis, you should draw a bar chart. The bars do not touch. When the x-axis has a continuous scale, you should draw a frequency diagram or histogram. The bars touch.

The variation that we can see or detect between living organisms is called **phenotypic variation**. It is caused by both genetic and environmental factors.

In general:

- Discontinuous variation is almost always caused by genes alone, for example human blood groups.
- Continuous variation is caused by an interaction between genes and environment, for example human height.

Mutation

Mutation is a change in a gene. Mutation produces new alleles of genes.

Definition
Mutation – genetic change.

Mutation can happen for no obvious reason, just by chance. But the risk of mutation happening is increased by some chemicals, and by ionising radiation.

We have seen that a gene is a section of DNA that codes for a protein, and the code is in the form of the sequence of bases in the DNA.

A mutation is a change in this sequence of bases. This means that the protein produced from these instructions is different. It has a different sequence of amino acids.

Definition
Mutation – a change in the base sequence of DNA.

Sickle cell anaemia

One important gene in human cells codes for the protein haemoglobin.

- Some people have an allele of this gene that has a changed base sequence.
- This faulty allele therefore results in haemoglobin with an incorrect amino acid sequence.
- The haemoglobin therefore cannot perform its function – transporting oxygen – properly.

A person with two copies of the faulty allele has a disease called sickle cell anaemia.

The normal allele can be represented by the symbol Hb^A and the faulty, sickle cell allele Hb^S.

Genotype	Phenotype
Hb^AHb^A	normal
Hb^AHb^S	sickle cell trait (carrier)
Hb^SHb^S	sickle cell anaemia

People with either one or two copies of the faulty allele have resistance to malaria. Malaria is a serious disease caused by a protoctist pathogen that is transmitted by mosquitoes. People with the sickle cell allele are therefore less likely to die from malaria than people who do not have this allele.

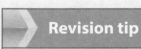

Revision tip

You may like to practise constructing genetic diagrams to show how the sickle cell allele can be inherited.

- In a country where there is no malaria, people with the sickle cell allele are at a disadvantage, because their blood does not carry oxygen very well. People without the sickle cell allele are more likely to survive to adulthood and have children. So most children will not inherit a sickle cell allele from their parents.
- In a country where malaria is common, many young children with the normal allele will die from malaria. Children with one copy of the sickle cell allele are more likely to survive to adulthood and have children of their own. So many children will inherit a sickle cell allele from their parents.

Adaptive features

Most of the features that are caused by genes help organisms to survive in their environment. For example, genes cause fish to grow fins and monkeys to grow legs. These are called **adaptive features**.

Definition

Adaptive feature – an inherited feature that helps an organism to survive and reproduce in its environment.

Supplement

Biologists use the term **fitness** to describe how well an organism is adapted to survive in its environment. The greater the fitness of an organism, the more likely it is to survive long enough to reproduce.

Definitions

Adaptive feature – the inherited functional features of an organism that increase its fitness.
Fitness – the probability of an organism surviving and reproducing in the environment in which it is found.

The diagrams show adaptive features of plants that live in wet places and in dry places.

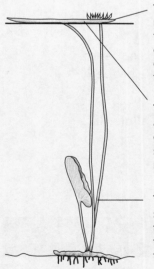

The stomata are on top of rather than underneath the leaves, so that carbon dioxide and oxygen can diffuse in and out from the air.

The leaves contain large air spaces, so that they can float on the water surface where there is most light.

The stems have air spaces, to help them to float and to allow oxygen to diffuse to all parts of the plant.

Water lilies are adapted to live in water. They are **hydrophytes**.

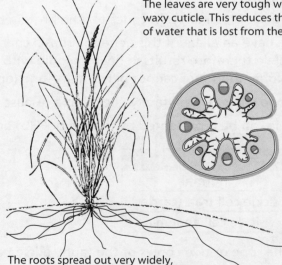

The leaves are very tough with a thick, waxy cuticle. This reduces the amount of water that is lost from the leaves.

The leaves can roll up with the stomata inside. This traps moist air. This reduces the water potential gradient between the inside and outside of the leaf, which reduces the rate of water loss by transpiration.

The roots spread out very widely, anchoring the plant in the dry, loose sand.

Marram grass is adapted to live in dry, sandy places. It is a **xerophyte**.

Selection

Natural selection

We have seen that organisms belonging to the same species vary from each other. Organisms with some variations may be better adapted to their environment. They may be more likely to survive and reproduce. So their alleles are the ones that are most likely to passed on to the next generation.

We can summarise how **natural selection** happens like this:

- Organisms have different combinations of alleles for the same feature. This produces variation within a population of organisms.
- Many kinds of organism can produce huge numbers of offspring. Many of these offspring will not survive to adulthood, because of competition with each other, or because they are killed by predators or disease. This is sometimes described as a 'struggle for survival'.
- The ones that are most likely to survive and reproduce are the ones that have alleles that make them better adapted to their environment.
- So the alleles that are passed on to the next generation are those that provide the best adaptation to the environment.

Revision tip

When you are writing about natural selection, never suggest that an organism changes so that it or its offspring become better adapted. Other organisms are no more able to do that than you are.

Selective breeding

Humans use a similar process to breed varieties of animals or crop plants to suit their purposes. For example:

- There is variation between maize plants. Some of the variation is because they have different alleles.
- We can choose two individual plants that have features that we want to make more of – for example, high yield and resistance to drought.
- We can breed the plant with a high yield with the plant with resistance to drought.
- We can then plant the seeds and let them grow into adult maize plants. We can choose the ones that have the highest yield and the best resistance to drought.
- We can cross these chosen plants, collect their seeds and grow them into adult plants.
- Again, we can choose the best plants to breed from.
- This will need to be done for several more generations.

Supplement

Evolution

Normally, natural selection keeps the same features in a population, generation after generation. This is because the organisms already have adaptive features that help them to survive.

However, if the environment changes – for example, if the climate gets hotter – then different features may give the best chance of survival. Organisms with these features now become the ones most likely to survive and reproduce. So, over time, the most common features in the population change. The population becomes better adapted to the new environment. We say that **evolution** has taken place.

> **Definition**
>
> **Process of adaptation** – the process, resulting from natural selection, by which populations become more suited to their environment over many generations.

An example of evolution by natural selection

Many human diseases are caused by bacteria. We can treat bacterial infections using antibiotics.

Within a population of bacteria, some may – just by chance – have alleles that make them resistant to antibiotics. When they do not come into contact with antibiotics, these bacteria are no more likely to survive and reproduce than any of the others. But if the bacteria come into contact with an antibiotic, then only the ones that happen to have the resistance allele will survive and reproduce.

So the next generation of bacteria will almost all have the resistance allele. An antibiotic-resistant strain of bacteria has been produced.

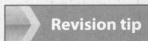

Revision tip

It is wrong to say that the bacteria are 'immune' to the antibiotic. Immunity involves the production of memory cells in the immune system.

Comparing natural selection and selective breeding (by artificial selection)

Both natural selection and selective breeding rely on genetic variation within a population.

In natural selection, it is the individuals with the variations that best adapt them to their environment that survive and reproduce. In selective breeding, it is the individuals with the variations that humans want that survive and reproduce.

In both cases, the next generation will inherit alleles from the selected parents, and so will have the adaptive or desired features.

In both cases, the selection process continues for many generations.

Quick test

1. Give one example of continuous variation.
2. What is the name of the process that forms new alleles of genes?
3. Define *adaptive feature*.
4. Describe two adaptive features of African lions.
5. Write the letters of these statements in the correct order, to explain how natural selection happens. Start with statement **E**.
   A Many offspring are produced.
   B They pass on their alleles to the next generation.
   C There is a struggle for survival between the young organisms.
   D Only those with alleles that provide the best adaptation to the environment survive long enough to reproduce.
   E There is genetic variation among the members of a population.

Supplement

6. What causes discontinuous variation?
7. Define *gene mutation*.
8. Use a genetic diagram to explain how two people who are carriers for sickle cell anaemia can have a child that has the disease.
9. Explain why sickle cell anaemia is most common in countries where malaria is common.
10. List **two** adaptive features of hydrophytes.

Biotechnology and genetic engineering

Biotechnology is the use of biological processes to make things that humans can use.

Using yeast

Yeast is a unicellular (one-celled) fungus. When yeast respires anaerobically, it produces **ethanol** and **carbon dioxide**.

glucose ⟶ ethanol + carbon dioxide

The glucose can come from sugar-containing waste substances from food manufacturing, or from the processing of maize grains.

Ethanol is used to make biofuels, which can be used instead of, or as well as, petrol (gasoline) in vehicles. A biofuel is a fuel that has been made by living organisms.

Carbon dioxide is used to make bread rise. When the bread is cooked, any ethanol that the yeast has made is destroyed.

Using pectinase

Pectinase is an enzyme that breaks down pectin. Pectin is a kind of 'glue' that holds plant cells together.

Adding pectinase to fruit makes it easier to crush the cells and extract juice. Pectinase also breaks down pectin in the juice, making it look less cloudy.

Using biological washing powders

A biological washing powder is one that contains enzymes. The enzymes are often extracted from bacteria that are adapted for living in hot springs. These enzymes have high optimum temperatures.

Biological washing powders may contain:

- protease to digest protein stains (for example haemoglobin from blood)
- lipase to digest fat stains (for example egg yolk)
- amylase to digest starch (for example from rice or bread).

The enzymes are usually mixed with detergents. Manufacturers will recommend a washing temperature that is not so high that it will denature the enzymes.

Supplement
Using lactase

Lactase is an enzyme that breaks down the disaccharide lactose, which is found in milk.

lactose ⟶ glucose + galactose

Human babies produce lactose in their digestive system, to digest lactose in milk. However, most adults stop producing lactase. If they drink milk or eat foods containing lactose, they cannot digest it and may feel ill.

Lactase can be added to milk to break down the lactose, producing lactose-free milk. This can be drunk by anyone, even if they do not make their own lactase.

Making penicillin

Penicillin a very useful antibiotic. It is used in the treatment of many bacterial infections.

Penicillin is made by a fungus called *Penicillium*. The fungus is grown in a **fermenter**. Nutrients and oxygen are supplied, and the fungus is grown for several days. The contents of the fermenter are then collected, and penicillin is extracted and purified.

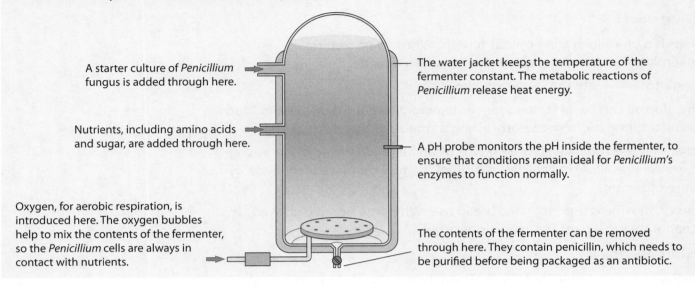

A starter culture of *Penicillium* fungus is added through here.

Nutrients, including amino acids and sugar, are added through here.

Oxygen, for aerobic respiration, is introduced here. The oxygen bubbles help to mix the contents of the fermenter, so the *Penicillium* cells are always in contact with nutrients.

The water jacket keeps the temperature of the fermenter constant. The metabolic reactions of *Penicillium* release heat energy.

A pH probe monitors the pH inside the fermenter, to ensure that conditions remain ideal for *Penicillium*'s enzymes to function normally.

The contents of the fermenter can be removed through here. They contain penicillin, which needs to be purified before being packaged as an antibiotic.

Genetic engineering

Genetic engineering is making changes to the genes in an organism, to give it features that we can make use of.

> **Definition**
>
> **Genetic engineering** – changing the genetic material of an organism by removing, changing or inserting individual genes.

For example:

- The human gene for **making insulin** can be removed from human cells and inserted into a bacterium's cell. The bacterium will divide repeatedly to form a whole population of bacteria containing the human gene. These bacteria will follow the instructions on the human gene and make insulin. This can be used for the treatment of people with diabetes.
- Genes that make plants **resistant to** (unaffected by) **herbicides** can be inserted into crop plants. This means that a farmer can spray the crop with herbicide to kill weeds, but the crop plant will not be affected.
- Genes that make **plants resistant to insect pest**s can be inserted into crop plants. The farmer does not need to spray pesticides on the crop, which now has its own in-built protection from them.
- Genes for **making vitamins** can be inserted into crop plants. The plants will make extra vitamins, which make them more nutritious for people to eat.

Bacteria are often used in biotechnology and genetic engineering because:

- they reproduce very rapidly;
- different kinds of bacteria can make many different kinds of complex molecules.

- No one minds what is done to bacteria, whereas there are ethical concerns about using animals such as sheep or even fish.
- Although bacteria are very simple, their genetic code is exactly the same as in other organisms, so they can follow the instructions on human genes, for example the gene for making human insulin.
- Bacteria have little circles of DNA called plasmids, which makes it easy to put genes from other organisms inside them.

How genetic engineering is done

Bacteria can be genetically engineered to make a human protein.

1. DNA is extracted from human cells. The DNA is cut into small pieces using **restriction enzymes**.

2. Restriction enzymes cut DNA at different places on the two strands, which leaves short lengths of unpaired bases at each end. These are called **sticky ends**.

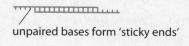

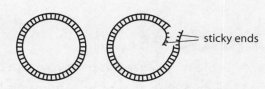

unpaired bases form 'sticky ends'

3. The same restriction enzymes are used to cut **plasmids** in bacteria. This opens up the circular plasmids, again leaving sticky ends. The sticky ends at one end of the cut human DNA and the sticky ends at one end of the opened-up plasmid have **complementary bases** to one another.

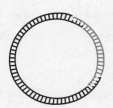

sticky ends

4. The cut human DNA and the cut plasmid are mixed together. The complementary bases on the two lots of sticky ends join together.

5. An enzyme called **DNA ligase** is mixed with the human DNA and plasmids. This enzyme joins the plasmids back together again into complete circles. The plasmids are now **recombinant** plasmids, because they contain genes from the bacterium and a human gene.

6. The recombinant plasmids are put into bacteria.

7. The bacteria are put into fermenters and allowed to reproduce. They produce whole populations of bacteria, each containing copies of the recombinant plasmids. They use the instructions on the human gene to make the protein that the gene codes for.

> **Revision tip**
>
> Once the bacteria have been genetically engineered, it doesn't need doing again. Each time they divide, the bacteria copy the human gene as well as their own, so all their descendants also contain the human gene.

Advantages and disadvantages of genetically modifying crops

Genetically engineered varieties of many different crop plants have now been produced. For example:

- a variety of rice has had genes added to it that cause it to make large amounts of vitamin A;
- a variety of maize has had genes added to it that allow it to make a toxin that kills pests that eat the grain;
- a variety of soya has had genes added to it that allow it to make a protein that gives it resistance to herbicides, so farmers can kill weeds without killing the soya plants.

Some advantages of this include:

- having extra vitamin A in rice makes it more nutritious, especially for children whose diets do not contain enough vitamin A and who are at risk of developing night blindness;

- crop plants that make their own toxins to kill insect pests do not need to be sprayed with insecticides. This reduces costs to the farmer and also reduces the risk that beneficial insects will be harmed;
- if crop plants are resistant to herbicides, farmers can kill weeds in the crop using that herbicide. This increases yields, so more crop can be harvested from the same area of land.

Some disadvantages of this include:

- seeds of genetically engineered crops can be more expensive than normal seeds, so some farmers might not be able to afford them;
- genetic engineering is a very technical process, requiring highly skilled people and high-quality laboratory facilities;
- some people are worried that eating genetically engineered crops might make them ill, so the farmer might not be able to sell his crop. (However, every food that we eat contains DNA, so eating food made from a genetically engineered crop plant isn't really any different from eating any crop plant.)

Quick test

1. Explain how yeast is used to make biofuels.
2. Explain how anaerobic respiration in yeast helps with making bread.
3. What is pectinase, and what is it used for?
4. Name **two** enzymes that may be found in biological washing powders.
5. Define *genetic engineering*.
6. Give **two** examples of genetic engineering in crop plants.

Supplement

7. How is lactose-free milk produced?
8. Name the fungus that makes penicillin.
9. Explain why the fermenters used for penicillin production are surrounded by a water jacket.
10. What is a plasmid?
11. What are sticky ends, and how are they formed?

Exam-style practice questions

1 **(a)** Define the terms *gene* and *mutation*. [3]

(b) In a species of animal, a gene determines the length of hair. Allele **A** is dominant and gives long hair. Allele **a** gives short hair.

    (i) Give the genotype of an animal with short hair. [1]

    (ii) Copy and complete the genetic diagram to predict the results of a cross between two heterozygous animals.

       Parental phenotypes ....

       Parental genotypes   Aa   Aa

       Gametes ◯ ◯   ◯ ◯

       Offspring genotypes and phenotypes

[4]

(c) A group of these animals, some with long hair and some with short hair, are introduced to an island in a very cold climate.
After many years, almost all of the animals in the population have long hair.
Explain how this could happen. [4]

2 **(a)** List **two** reasons why bacteria are useful in biotechnology. [2]

(b) Anaerobic respiration in yeast is used in the production of biofuels.

    (i) Write the word equation for anaerobic respiration in yeast. [2]

    (ii) Explain what is meant by a biofuel. [1]

    (iii) State the product of anaerobic respiration in yeast that is used to make biofuels. [1]

    (iv) Outline **one** other way in which we make use of anaerobic respiration in yeast. [2]

Supplement

3 **(a)** Explain the importance of the sequence of bases in DNA for determining the features of a cell or organism. [4]

(b) When two gametes fuse, a zygote is formed with one set of chromosomes from the father and one from the mother.

   (i) Name the type of cell division that is used to produce gametes. [1]

   (ii) The zygote divides by mitosis to produce all of the cells in the new organism's body. Outline how mitosis ensures that all of these cells have full sets of chromosomes. [2]

(c) Although every cell in the body has the same chromosomes and genes, cells in different tissues have very different features.

   (i) Give **one** example of a specialised cell, and state **one** feature that is not found in other specialised cells. [1]

   (ii) Explain why cells with the same chromosomes and genes can develop different features. [2]

   (iii) Stem cells do not become specialised. Explain the importance of stem cells in the body. [2]

4 **(a)** Outline the uses of the following enzymes in genetic engineering:

   (i) Restriction enzymes; [2]

   (ii) DNA ligase. [2]

(b) Maize is an important food crop in many countries. Varieties of maize that are tolerant to drought have been produced by genetic engineering and also by selective breeding.

   (i) Outline how selective breeding could be used to produce drought-tolerant maize. [5]

   (ii) Suggest advantages of producing drought-tolerant maize by selective breeding, rather than by genetic engineering. [2]

Energy flow in ecosystems

All organisms need energy to maintain the metabolic reactions that keep them alive. The energy that organisms use originally comes from the Sun, as sunlight. Plants use this energy for photosynthesis.

Supplement

- Energy from sunlight is used by plants in photosynthesis. Some of the energy is trapped as chemical energy inside the carbohydrates and other organic substances that they make.
- Other organisms get their energy by eating plants, or by eating animals that have eaten plants.
- Eventually, all of this energy is returned to the environment in the form of heat.

Food chains and webs

A **food chain** is a diagram that shows how energy passes from one organism to another. Energy passes into a plant when it uses sunlight in photosynthesis. Energy passes into an animal when it ingests its food.

$$\text{producer} \longrightarrow \begin{matrix}\text{primary}\\\text{consumer}\end{matrix} \longrightarrow \begin{matrix}\text{secondary}\\\text{consumer}\end{matrix} \longrightarrow \begin{matrix}\text{tertiary}\\\text{consumer}\end{matrix}$$

Primary consumers are also called **herbivores**. Secondary and tertiary consumers are **carnivores**.

All the organisms in a food chain produce waste products, and all of them eventually die. The energy in their waste products and dead bodies is used by **decomposers**.

Most organisms feed on many different producers or consumers, so that many different food chains interconnect. A diagram showing interconnecting food chains is called a **food web**.

> ### Revision tip
>
> Although it is true that the arrows in a food chain show 'what eats what', this is not a good enough answer at IGCSE® level. The arrows show the direction of energy flow.

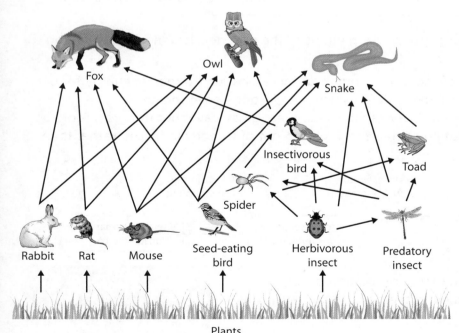

We can use a food web to predict what might happen if human activities affect the food web.

For example:

- If humans killed and ate all the rabbits, then the foxes might have less food and their numbers might decrease. However, the foxes might just eat more rats, mice and birds. This might reduce the populations of these prey species. This might mean that there would be less food for owls, so their numbers might reduce.
- If humans introduced a new kind of predator, it might compete with foxes, owls and snakes for food, so their populations would decrease.

Definitions

Food chain – a diagram showing the transfer of energy from one organism to the next, beginning with a producer.

Food web – a network of interconnected food chains.

Producer – an organism that makes its own organic nutrients, usually using energy from sunlight, through photosynthesis.

Consumer – an organism that gets its energy by feeding on other organisms.

Herbivore – an animal that gets its energy by eating plants.

Carnivore – an animal that gets its energy by eating other animals.

Decomposer – an organism that gets its energy from dead or waste organic material.

Supplement

Each stage in a food chain is called a **trophic level**. Energy is transferred between trophic levels as chemical energy in organic nutrients (carbohydrates, fats and proteins) in food.

Definition

Trophic level – the position of an organism in a food chain, food web, pyramid of numbers or pyramid of biomass.

The amount of energy passing from one group of organisms to the next gets less the further you go along a food chain. This happens because:

- Each organism breaks down some of the organic nutrients by respiration, to release energy for use in its body. Some of this energy is wasted as heat, which goes into the environment.
- Not all parts of an organism are eaten – for example, zebras eat grass leaves but not grass roots.
- Some of the energy in the food that an animal eats is passed out of its body in faeces, rather than becoming part of its body.

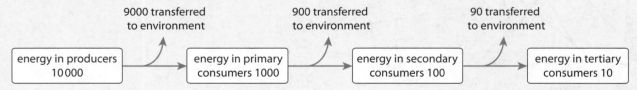

The **efficiency** of energy transfer is a measure of the proportion of energy in one trophic level that is passed to the next trophic level. This is often about 10%.

The more energy there is in a trophic level, the more organisms can exist at that trophic level. By the time you get to a fifth trophic level in a food chain – the quaternary consumers – there is very little energy left. This means that any animals feeding at this trophic level will be very rare.

Pyramids of numbers

We can show the numbers of organisms at different trophic levels in a food chain by drawing a **pyramid of numbers**. The size of each bar represents the number of organisms at that level.

trophic level 4: tertiary consumers

trophic level 3: secondary consumers

trophic level 2: primary consumers

trophic level 1: producers

> **Revision tip**

Always draw a pyramid of numbers using rectangular bars. Do not draw a triangle. This is because the area of the bars represents the number of organisms. It is a bit like a sideways-on bar chart.

Supplement

Pyramids of biomass

Some pyramids of numbers may look an odd shape. For example, if a tree is the producer, there might be only one tree and thousands of insects feeding on its leaves. This would make a pyramid with a tiny bar for the producers and a very large bar for the primary consumers.

However, if we draw a **pyramid of biomass**, the pyramid will have a shape like the one shown above. Instead of numbers of organisms, we use the bars to represent the mass of the organisms at each trophic level.

Efficiency of eating crop plants or animal products

On a given area of land, there is more energy contained in a crop of plants grown on that land, than there would be in a herd of animals grazing on the land. So, in theory, humans could get more energy and sustain a larger population if we ate crop plants rather than eating animals or animal products such as milk and eggs.

Quick test

1. Water plants are eaten by snails, which are eaten by snail kites. Show this as a food chain.
2. What do the arrows in this food chain represent?
3. Name the producer in this food chain.
4. Draw a pyramid of numbers for this food chain.
5. Explain how energy from this food chain can be passed to decomposers.

Supplement

6. In what form is energy when (a) it enters a food chain and (b) it is passed along the chain?
7. Explain why energy transfer along a food chain is inefficient.
8. What is the meaning of the term *trophic level*?
9. Explain why food chains generally have fewer than five trophic levels.

Nutrient cycles

The molecules from which the bodies of living organisms are made contain several different elements. Atoms of these elements move between the organisms in an ecosystem, and the air, water and soil, in a continuous cycle.

The carbon cycle

The diagram shows how carbon atoms move between different organisms and their environment. This is called the **carbon cycle**.

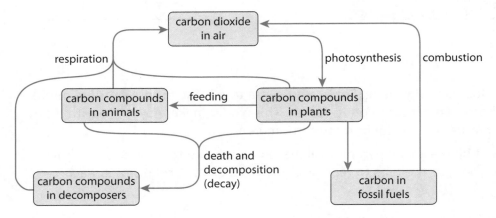

- Fossil fuels take millions of years to form. This happened long ago. When we burn fossil fuels, the carbon in them changes to carbon dioxide and goes into the air. This increases the quantity of carbon dioxide in the atmosphere.
- Trees take more carbon dioxide from the air in photosynthesis than they put back through respiration. If we cut down huge numbers of trees, there is less photosynthesis and so less carbon dioxide is removed from the air. If we burn the trees, then the carbon in their bodies is returned to the air as carbon dioxide.

The water cycle

All living organisms need water. The diagram shows the water cycle.

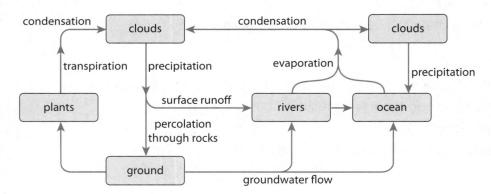

The nitrogen cycle

The diagram shows how nitrogen atoms are cycled between organisms and their environment.

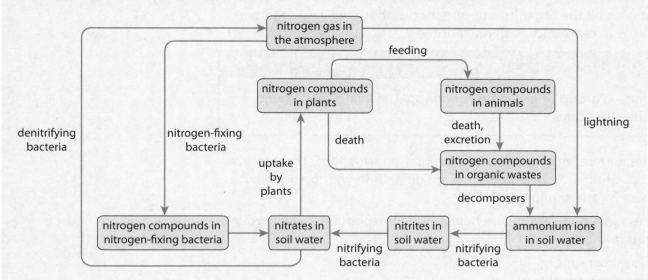

- Nitrogen in the air is in the form of nitrogen molecules, N_2. These are very stable and unreactive. Animals and plants cannot use N_2.
- Changing N_2 into a more reactive form that plants can use is called **nitrogen fixation**. This can be done by lightning and nitrogen-fixing bacteria. Lightning causes nitrogen and water in the air to combine to form **nitrate ions**, NO_3^-. Nitrogen-fixing bacteria change nitrogen gas to **ammonium ions**, NH_4^+.
- In the soil nitrifying bacteria change ammonium ions to nitrate ions. This is called **nitrification**.
- Plants can take up ammonium ions and nitrate ions through their roots. They use them to make amino acids. These are then used to make proteins.
- Animals eat plants. They digest proteins to amino acids and then build them up into different proteins.
- Dead animals and plants, and their waste products, contain proteins and amino acids. These are broken down by decomposers to produce ammonium ions. This is called **deamination**.
- Another group of bacteria in the soil break down nitrate ions to produce nitrogen gas. This is called **denitrification**.

Quick test

1. Name one carbon-containing compound found in the tissues of an animal.
2. Name the process that removes carbon dioxide from the air.
3. Explain why combustion of fossil fuels increases the concentration of carbon dioxide in the air.
4. Name the process by which water vapour turns to liquid water.
5. In the water cycle, in what state is water (a) in clouds and (b) as it is lost from plants?

Supplement

6. Name one nitrogen-containing compound found in animals.
7. Explain why plants and animals cannot use nitrogen gas from the air.
8. Describe **two** ways in which nitrogen fixation takes place.
9. Outline the role of nitrifying bacteria in the nitrogen cycle.
10. Decomposers break down amino acids to produce ammonium ions. What is the name of this process?

Populations

A population is all the organisms of one species that are living together. They are able to reproduce with one another.

Definition
Population – a group of organisms of one species living in the same area at the same time.

Usually, the number of organisms in a population stays fairly constant over long periods of time. The numbers may go up and down (fluctuate) but overall there is little change.

The numbers in a population, and how quickly the population can grow, are reduced if:

- food is in short supply;
- there are many predators;
- there are serious diseases present.

The human population

The graph shows how the human population on Earth has changed over the last 10 000 years.

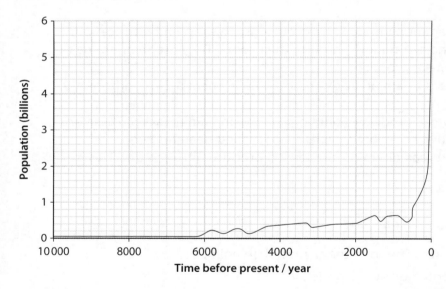

Human population growth has been very rapid over the last 250 years. This is a result of changes such as:

- better access to medical treatment
- a better diet
- more access to clean water supplies.

This rapid growth in our population has many social and environmental implications. These include:

- more demand for limited resources, such as water, land or food supplies; this can result in conflict;
- more pollution, for example more carbon dioxide added to the atmosphere and more raw sewage entering waterways;

- more crowded living conditions for many people, so pathogens can spread more rapidly;
- increased loss of habitats for other living organisms, as people use more land for building cities or producing crops.

Supplement

Communities and ecosystems

Populations do not live in isolation. Each habitat (place where organisms live) contains many different populations of many different species. All the populations living in the same place at the same time make up a **community**.

Communities of organisms interact with their environment. They affect the soil, water and air where they live, and these non-living things also affect the organisms. This interaction between all the living things in an area and their non-living environment is called an **ecosystem**.

We can think of an ecosystem on many different scales. The surface of a rotting orange is an ecosystem, made up of the orange and all the different kinds of fungi and bacteria that are growing on it, as well as the air around them. A lake is an ecosystem, made up of all the living things in the lake, plus the water in the lake, the mud on the bottom of the lake and the gases dissolved in the water.

Definitions

Community – all of the populations of different species in an ecosystem.
Ecosystem – a unit containing the community of organisms and their environment, interacting together, for example a decomposing log or a lake.

The sigmoid population growth curve

Imagine that a small number of organisms of a particular species is introduced to a new environment – for example, a few yeast cells added to a flask containing sugar solution, or a few rabbits introduced to an island. If we count their numbers over the next few days (for the yeast cells) or years (for the rabbits) we often find that the size of the population follows the same pattern. This is shown in the graph.

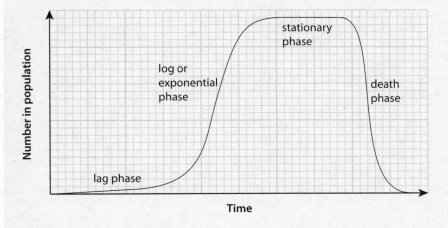

During the **lag phase**, organisms are settling into their new environment. Yeast cells may need to begin to synthesise the appropriate enzymes to help them to feed on the nutrients they have been provided with. Rabbits may need to find suitable places to make burrows and feed, or learn how to avoid predators in their new environment.

During the **log** or **exponential phase**, organisms reproduce rapidly. They have plenty of resources available to them. There are no limiting factors. Their birth rate is much greater than the death rate.

Eventually, however, the population gets so large that resources begin to be in short supply. The yeast cells in their flask begin to run out of nutrients and oxygen. Their toxic waste products build up. The rabbits may run out of suitable places to make burrows, and there may not be enough food to supply more rabbits. There is **competition** for resources. Disease may begin to spread more widely. All of these act as **limiting factors**, preventing further growth. The habitat has reached its **carrying capacity**. Population growth therefore slows down and stops, as death rate becomes equal to birth rate. This is the **stationary phase**.

For most populations, this is the final phase of the population growth curve. The population remains at a fairly steady level, but probably fluctuating up and down from year to year. For the yeast, however, trapped in its flask, once it has used up the nutrients it stops reproducing. Now death rate is much greater than birth rate, and the population size rapidly falls. This is the **death phase**.

Quick test

1. Define *population*.
2. List **three** factors that affect the rate of population growth.
3. List **two** social or environmental consequences of the current rate of human population growth.

Supplement

4. Define *ecosystem*.
5. Explain what is meant by a sigmoid population growth curve.
6. Look at the graph showing human population growth. Identify the phase of population growth that we are currently experiencing.
7. Imagine that a small number of a species of fish are introduced to a lake.
   (a) Explain why their numbers may increase exponentially for the first few years.
   (b) Explain why the growth of their population will eventually stop.

Human influences on ecosystems

Food supply

The food that we eat is supplied from farms and gardens. Modern technology has increased the quantity of food that can be obtained from a given area of land.

- **Agricultural machinery**, such as tractors, allows a farmer to do much more work on the land in a day than using hand tools, or machinery pulled by animals.
- **Chemical fertilisers** containing mineral ions such as nitrate provide extra nutrients to growing crop plants. They grow faster and larger, and produce greater yields.
- **Insecticides** – chemicals that kill insects – can be sprayed onto growing crops to kill pests that feed on the plants. This increases the yield from the crop.
- **Herbicides** – chemicals that kill plants – can be sprayed onto the crop to kill weeds. This reduces competition between the weeds and the crop plant for resources such as light and water, so the crop plants can grow faster and larger, increasing yield.
- **Selective breeding** (see page 109) has produced new varieties of animals (including cattle, fish and poultry) and crop plants that grow faster and are able to survive better in difficult conditions, such as in times of drought.

Negative impacts of farming on ecosystems

A field of maize, sorghum or rice contains just a single kind of plant. This is called a **monoculture**. Few other organisms can live there. The number of different species is therefore very small, compared with a natural ecosystem. Large-scale monocultures covering huge areas of land – such as a huge rubber plantation or vast fields of wheat – can completely destroy the natural ecosystem in that area.

Livestock (such as cattle, sheep or goats) can also pose threats to an ecosystem. If the number of livestock is quite low, then they may not do too much harm. But if large numbers of livestock are kept in a small area (known as intensive livestock production) they may **overgraze** the land. The plants are eaten faster than they can regrow. The soil becomes exposed to wind and rain, and may be eroded. Faeces from the animals may build up, spreading disease among them and polluting waterways.

Supplement

Famine

The more the human population grows, the more food we need to produce, and the greater the impact on the environment.

In some places, it may not be possible to provide enough food for all the people who live there. This causes **famine**.

Famine happens as a result of:

- extreme weather events such as drought or flooding; these may become more common as global warming increases;

- growth in the human population outstripping growth in food production;
- poverty preventing people from buying seeds, tools, fertilisers or machinery to help them to work the land and grow crops;
- unequal distribution of food, so that even though there is enough food produced for everyone, many people still do not get enough.

Habitat destruction

A habitat is a place where organisms live.

Humans destroy habitats:

- to provide more land for farming and housing;
- to extract natural resources, such as minerals or fossil fuels;
- by adding pollutants to the environment, for example sewage or oil in the sea.

Human activities can also damage food webs, for example by killing some species, or introducing new ones. (See page 118.)

Deforestation has particularly large effects. Deforestation means cutting down large areas of trees. The table summarises some of the harmful effects of deforestation.

Effect	Explanation (Supplement)
loss of habitat	Plants and animals that live in forests have adaptations that allow them to live there. They may not survive when the forest is cut down, and this could result in extinction of species.
loss of soil	Plant roots help to hold soil in place, especially on slopes. When trees are lost, soil is easily eroded by wind or water.
increased flooding	Rain falling onto a forest hits leaves before it hits the ground, so it can be steadily absorbed into the soil. With no trees, rain water hits the ground directly, and is likely to run off rather than soak gently into the soil. Moreover, there are no tree roots to take up water from the ground.
increased carbon dioxide in the atmosphere	No trees means less photosynthesis to remove carbon dioxide from the air. If the trees are burnt, this produces more carbon dioxide.

Pollution

Land and water pollution

Insecticides used by farmers on crops may kill beneficial insects, such as bees that act as pollinators. This can slow down reproduction of plants with insect-pollinated flowers. It may also reduce food supplies for animals that feed on insects, so their populations may fall.

Herbicides used by farmers on crops to kill weeds may kill other plants as well, or they may be harmful to insects.

Insecticides or herbicides may be washed into rivers, lakes or the sea by rainfall, where they may harm aquatic (water-living) organisms.

Nuclear fallout is radioactive material that is produced by nuclear weapons, or by accidents at nuclear plants for generating electricity. Radioactivity causes radiation burns, radiation sickness and mutations. It remains in the environment for a very long time.

Chemical waste, for example from factories, may contain toxins (poisons) such as heavy metals, which harm living organisms. **Discarded rubbish** may also contain toxins, and always looks very unsightly.

Untreated sewage may contain pathogens from humans, and so can spread diseases such as cholera or polio.

Both untreated sewage and **fertilisers** contain nutrients that increase plant growth if they enter rivers, lakes or the sea. This can cause **algal blooms**. The algae may produce toxins that can kill animals that drink the water.

Supplement

When fertiliser or untreated sewage enters a body of water, a sequence of events called **eutrophication** takes place.

1. The extra nutrients, such as nitrates, means that producers such as aquatic plants and algae grow faster, because nutrients are no longer limiting their population growth. They may completely cover the water surface.
2. The producers on the water surface prevent light reaching plants growing below them, so they cannot photosynthesise and die.
3. The dead plants provide food for decomposers. The numbers of decomposers therefore increase.
4. Many decomposers (for example bacteria) respire aerobically. They use up most of the oxygen dissolved in the water.
5. Animals in the water now do not have enough oxygen. They may move away, or die.

Non-biodegradable plastics are plastics that cannot be broken down by decomposers. When they have been thrown away, they remain in the environment for a very long time. They can cause harm to living organisms. Land animals, such as mice, may enter plastic bottles and get trapped. Sea turtles mistake them for jellyfish and eat them. This can block the alimentary canals of the turtles so that they cannot absorb nutrients, and eventually die.

Female contraceptive hormones may also get into rivers, lakes or the sea. They can cause feminisation in some aquatic animals. For example, male fish may become female. Exposure to water containing these hormones can also reduce sperm count in men.

Greenhouse gases and climate change

Greenhouse gases trap heat in the Earth's atmosphere. The two most important greenhouse gases are **carbon dioxide** and **methane**. Carbon dioxide is produced when fossil fuels are burnt. Methane is found in leakages of natural gas. It is produced by micro-organisms that break down rubbish, and in the intestines of cattle.

The concentrations of both of these greenhouse gases in the atmosphere are increasing. This is causing the temperatures on Earth to increase, leading to climate change.

Supplement

- Carbon dioxide and methane in the atmosphere allow short-wave radiation from the Sun to pass through to the ground.
- This radiation heats the ground, and is re-emitted as longer-wave radiation (infra-red).
- The longer-wave radiation cannot pass through the carbon dioxide and methane in the atmosphere, so it does not return to space.
- The longer-wave radiation is absorbed by the carbon dioxide and methane, raising the temperature of the atmosphere. Some of it is also reflected back to the ground.

This is called the **enhanced greenhouse effect**. It is causing a gradual increase in the mean temperatures on Earth.

Acid rain

Air pollution is also caused by **sulfur dioxide**. This gas dissolves in water droplets in clouds, making the water acidic. The **acid rain** that falls from these clouds decreases the pH of the water in rivers and lakes, killing animals and plants. It also damages trees, which may not be able to absorb minerals from the acidified soil.

Sulfur dioxide is produced when fossil fuels – especially coal – are burnt. We can reduce its production by:

- reducing the use of coal for electricity generation, for example by using oil instead or by using renewable energy (wind or solar);
- using 'scrubbers' to extract sulfur dioxide from waste gases before they are released into the environment.

Conservation

Conservation means caring for the environment.

Sustainable resources

Some of these resources, such as fossil fuels, are **non-renewable**. This means that we are using them up faster than they are produced, so they will eventually run out. If we want to carry on using these resources, we must **conserve** them – that is, we must take care not to use them up too quickly.

Some resources are **renewable**. If we do not use them up too quickly, they will not run out. For example, if we plant a tree for every tree that we cut down, then we will not run out of trees. If we do not take too many fish from the sea, the fish will be able to reproduce fast enough to replace the ones we have harvested. They are **sustainable** resources.

> **Definition**
>
> **Sustainable resource** – one that is produced as rapidly as it is removed from the environment, so that it does not run out.

Supplement

We can ensure that our use of forests is sustainable by:

- replanting at least one tree for every tree that is cut down;
- leaving enough of the trunk to allow the tree to regrow (coppicing or pollarding);
- only cutting down some trees (selective felling) so that the forest can regenerate from seeds produced by the remaining trees.

We can ensure that our harvesting of fish from the sea, rivers or lakes is sustainable by:

- drawing up international agreements about where different countries are allowed to fish, and how many fish they can take;
- limiting the areas (for example to avoid breeding areas) and the times (to avoid breeding seasons) that fishermen are allowed to take fish;
- imposing quotas – that is, limiting the number of fish that each boat or fisherman is allowed to catch;
- limiting the number of people or boats that can fish, for example by using a licencing or permit system;
- ensuring that nets have a wide mesh, so that young fish can escape and later reproduce;

- using patrol boats to ensure that fishing boats are obeying the rules and imposing severe penalties for breaking the rules;
- reducing demand for wild fish, for example by encouraging fish farming;
- educating people about fish stocks, so that they understand the importance of conserving them;
- breeding fish to increase numbers and then releasing them into the environment (restocking).

Recycling

We can reduce the quantity of resources that we take from the Earth by recycling. For example:

- used paper can be pulped and treated to remove ink; it can then be made into paper again;
- used glass can be smashed and melted, and then made into glass again;
- metals such as iron, zinc and aluminium can be melted and reformed into new metal objects;
- we can reuse plastic objects such as bottles; some kinds of plastics can be turned into other materials, such as fleece fabrics to make clothing.

All of this helps to reduce our need to extract materials from the Earth. However, they all use energy for transport costs and treating the used materials, so we need to consider whether the advantages of recycling outweigh the disadvantages of extra fuel use.

Water can also be recycled. **Sewage** can be treated to make it safe to return to waterways. Micro-organisms in the sewage treatment plant break down organic substances in the sewage. The treated sewage will not cause pollution, nor does it contain pathogens that will make people ill.

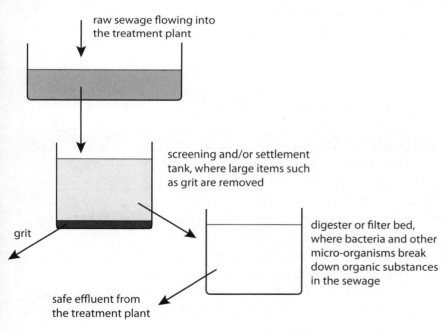

raw sewage flowing into the treatment plant

screening and/or settlement tank, where large items such as grit are removed

grit

digester or filter bed, where bacteria and other micro-organisms break down organic substances in the sewage

safe effluent from the treatment plant

Conserving endangered species

An endangered species is one that is at risk of becoming extinct. The table lists reasons for this, and some examples.

Reason for a species becoming endangered	Example
climate change	polar bears – loss of ice in the Arctic, so they can no longer hunt seals under the ice
human destruction of habitat	orang-utans – deforestation to allow the planting of rubber trees
hunting	Arabian oryx – hunted almost to extinction
pollution	sea turtles – killed by eating discarded plastics
introduced species	kiwis and other flightless birds in New Zealand – eggs eaten by rats

Supplement

Once the numbers of a species fall below a certain limit, it becomes more difficult for the species to survive. This is because the variety of alleles in the population is decreased. This loss of genetic variation makes it difficult for the species to adapt to changing environmental conditions through natural selection.

Humans can try to conserve species that are at risk of becoming extinct.
This can be done by:

- monitoring and protecting species in their habitats – for example, setting up reserves where habitats are not destroyed and animals cannot be hunted;
- education – teaching people about the importance of conserving their environment and how to care for it;
- captive breeding programmes – breeding endangered species in a safe environment such as a zoo, and then releasing some of the animals back into a protected habitat;
- seed banks – keeping seeds of species in controlled conditions, so that they can be used to keep the species in existence if it is threatened in the wild.

Supplement

The table summarises the reasons for setting up conservation programmes.

Reason	Explanation
reducing extinction	The loss of one species could have significant effects on food webs, perhaps causing many other species to become extinct.
protecting vulnerable environments	Pollution and the destruction of habitats can destroy environments such as wetlands. Whole communities of organisms adapted to live in these vulnerable habitats may then become extinct.
nutrient cycling and provision of resources	Humans take many resources from the environment. These include plants and animals for food; plants as sources of drugs; wood for fuel. We can also make use of genes in wild plants to breed new features into our crop plants. Conserving the environment means that we can continue to find and use these resources.

Sustainable development

As the human population continues to increase, we need to try to develop in ways that will allow all of these people to get enough food and water, have somewhere to live, and receive medical treatment. We must try to do this in ways that do not harm the environment.

Sustainable development – development providing for the needs of an increasing human population without harming the environment.

Sustainable development often involves **conflicting demands**. For example, people need water, but if we take too much water from a river we may destroy the organisms that live in the river. People need houses, but if we build houses on land where rare species live, we may make that species extinct.

Sustainable development therefore requires much careful thought and planning. At a local and national level, it involves **cooperation** between the developers and people who understand why the environment should be cared for. At an international level, it involves **international agreements** about development policies, and perhaps financial aid to encourage the type of development that provides both for people to live better lives, and for long-term damage to the environment to be avoided.

Quick test

1. List **two** ways in which modern technology has helped to increase food production.
2. What is a monoculture?
3. List **three** reasons for habitat destruction by humans.
4. State **one** source of the air pollutant methane.
5. Describe the effect of increasing carbon dioxide levels in the atmosphere.
6. Define *sustainable resource*.

Supplement

7. What is meant by the term *non-biodegradable*?
8. Outline the cause of acid rain.
9. State **one** effect of pollution by female contraceptive hormones.
10. Explain why a species is at increased risk of extinction if its population size becomes very small.

1   The diagram shows part of the carbon cycle.

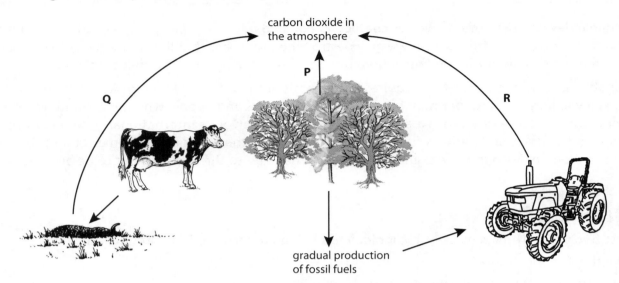

(a) (i)   Give the letter that represents combustion.   [1]

(ii) State what is represented by letter **P**.   [1]

(iii) Give the letter that represents respiration by decomposers.   [1]

(b) (i)   With reference to the diagram, explain why cutting down large areas of trees increases the concentration of carbon dioxide in the atmosphere.   [2]

(ii) List **two** other undesirable effects of cutting down forests.   [2]

(c)   Explain how the use of agricultural machinery has increased food production.   [2]

2   Aardvarks are mammals that eat ants and termites. Ants and termites feed on the seeds of grass plants. Gazelles also feed on grass. Hyenas and cheetahs feed on aardvarks and gazelles.

(a) (i)   Construct a food web to show the feeding relationships between these **seven** organisms. Use arrows to show the direction of energy flow.   [2]

(ii) Name the producer in the food web.   [1]

(iii) Explain how energy is transferred from one organism to another in the food web. [2]

(iv) State the principal source of energy input to the food web.   [1]

(b) Cheetahs are the most endangered big cat in Africa.

(i)   Suggest **two** possible reasons that cheetahs have become endangered.   [2]

(ii) Explain how zoos can help to conserve endangered species such as cheetahs.   [3]

Supplement

3 **(a) (i)** Explain why plants need nitrate ions. [2]

(ii) In tropical ecosystems, lightning during thunderstorms is often an important way in which nitrate ions are added to the soil.
Describe how this happens. [2]

(iii) Describe **one** process, other than lightning, that adds nitrate ions to the soil. [2]

(b) Where soil does not contain many nitrate ions, farmers can increase yields by adding fertiliser to their crops. Some of the fertiliser may be washed off the land and into rivers. Describe and explain the harmful effects that can result from this. [5]

4 The diagram shows a pyramid of energy for a forest ecosystem. The number in the bottom box indicates the quantity of energy, in arbitrary units, in this group of organisms.

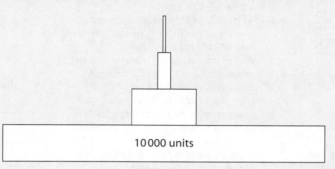

10 000 units

(a) Make a copy of the pyramid of energy. On the diagram:

(i) Label the **four** trophic levels. [1]

(ii) Suggest a value for the quantity of energy in the uppermost box on the diagram. [1]

(iii) Use the diagram, and your knowledge of energy transfer in food chains, to explain why food chains normally have fewer than five trophic levels. [3]

(b) Forests are used by humans for many different purposes.

(i) With reference to forests, explain what is meant by a *sustainable resource*. [3]

(ii) Discuss the reasons for conserving forests. [5]

Answers

How to use the exam practice mark schemes

; indicates a point worth one mark;
<u>underline</u> means that this specific term is required in order to get the mark;
ref. means reference to – note the reference must be in an appropriate context, so just the word alone will not earn a mark;
/ indicates alternative answers that can be awarded the mark;
, indicates which parts of the answer the / refers to. For example, in the marking point : kinetic energy of, enzymes and substrates/reactants, increases with temperature;
a correct answer requires reference to kinetic energy, plus either enzymes and substrates or reactants, plus increases with temperature.

1 Classification and cells

Classification of living organisms

1. Refer to the list on page 7.
2. *Ursus maritimus*.
3. In the plant kingdom, cells have cell walls and often have chloroplasts and large vacuoles. In the animal kingdom, cells do not have these features.
4. Amphibians have a smooth skin, but reptiles have scaly skin. Amphibians lay shell-less eggs in water, but reptiles lay eggs with rubbery shells on land.
5. Jointed legs ; hard exoskeleton ; segmented bodies.
6. How similar the sequence of bases in their DNA is ; how similar the sequence of amino acids in their proteins is ; how similar their morphology is ; how similar their anatomy is.
7. Protoctist.
8. Flowering plants ; dicotyledons.

Cells, tissues and organs

1. Cell membrane ; cytoplasm ; nucleus.
2. Cell membrane: controls the movement of substances into and out of the cell. Cytoplasm: where metabolic reactions take place. Nucleus: contains chromosomes made of DNA, which control the activities of the cell.
3. Transport of oxygen.
4. Photosynthesis.
5. A group of cells with similar structures, working together to perform a shared function.
6. ×3.

7. Animal cells and plant cells (and also fungal cells).
8. Aerobic respiration – the release of energy from nutrients.
9. All cells (including bacterial cells).
10. The site of protein synthesis.
11. 10 µm.

Diffusion, osmosis and active transport

1. Osmosis.
2. Cell membrane.
3. The cells lose water by osmosis. The tissue shrinks and loses mass.
4. Active transport.
5. The kinetic energy of the particles (molecules or ions).
6. At higher temperatures, kinetic energy of particles is greater, so the rate of diffusion increases.
7. Water moves down a water potential gradient from the soil into root hair cells, through their partially permeable cell membranes.
8. The pressure of the cell contents pushing outwards on the cell wall of a plant cell ; it helps to provide support for the soft tissues of the plant (such as in leaves).
9. The movement of glucose from the alimentary canal into the blood ; the movement of glucose from kidney tubules into the blood.

Biological molecules

1. Nitrogen.
2. Glucose.
3. Add biuret solution. If the solution contains protein, it will become purple.
4. Testing for vitamin C.
5. They increase the rate of metabolic reactions, which are essential for maintaining life.
6. Activity increases as temperature increases, up to the optimum (which is often – but not always – around 40 °C). Above the optimum temperature, enzyme activity decreases.
7. As a solvent to allow enzymes to digest nutrients ; as a solvent to allow the removal of waste materials such as urea in excretion ; as a solvent to transport materials in blood.
8. The sequence of amino acids determines the shape of the protein molecule. Enzymes are proteins. Enzymes that have different amino acid sequences have differently shaped active sites. Substrates can only bind with active sites that have a complementary shape. Therefore, enzymes with different amino

acid sequences bind with different substrates and catalyse different reactions.
9. As temperature increases, kinetic energy of enzyme and substrate molecules increases, so there are more successful collisions and the rate of reaction increases. At temperatures above the optimum temperature, the enzyme molecule begins to lose its shape, becoming denatured. The substrate can no longer bind with the active site, and the rate of reaction decreases.

Exam-style practice questions

1. (a) (i) Arthropod: jointed limbs/ segmented body/exoskeleton ; crustacean: more than four pairs of limbs/two pairs of antennae ; [2]
   (ii) *Homarus* ; [1]
   (b) *Any two of:* Compare their observable features to decide how similar they are ; determine whether they can breed together ; to produce fertile offspring ; [2]
   (c) (i) *Any two of:* Cells have cell walls ; cells have chloroplasts ; cells have large vacuoles ; [2]
   (ii) Tissue ; [1]
   (iii) 75/800 = 0.094 [2]
2. (a) (i) Net movement of particles ; from a region of their higher concentration to region of their lower concentration/ down a concentration gradient ; as a result of their random movement ; [3]
   (ii) *Any two of:* Movement is up a concentration gradient/ from low concentration to high concentration ; requires energy input from the cell ; only occurs across cell membranes ; [2]
   (b) (i) Orange/brown ; [1]
   (ii) Blue-black ; [1]
   (c) Oxygen diffuses into cells ; for respiration ; or carbon dioxide diffuses out of cells ; as a waste product of respiration ; or carbon dioxide diffuses into plant cells ; used in photosynthesis ; [2]
3. (a) B: mitochondrion ; D: endoplasmic reticulum ; [2]
   (b) Reference to energy release/ provide energy (not 'produce' energy) ; by respiration ; sperm cells need more energy than egg cells because they swim to egg ; [3]
   (c) (i) Controls activity of the cell ; [1]

(ii) Compare base sequences (in the DNA) ; the more similar the base sequences, the more closely related the organisms ; [2]

(d) Magnification = ×6556
59/0.009 [2]

4. (a) The net movement of water molecules ; from a region of higher water potential (dilute solution) to a region of lower water potential (concentrated solution) ; through a partially permeable membrane ; [3]

(b) (Osmosis is a type of diffusion and) the energy for this process is the kinetic energy of the molecules ; water molecules move faster at higher temperatures ; [2]

(c) Water potential is lower inside root hair cells than in the soil ; water moves into the cell down its water potential gradient ; through the partially permeable cell membrane ; [3]

(d) *Any four of:* Cells have lost water ; water cannot be taken up because water potential in soil is lower than water potential in root hair cells ; volume of cells decreases ; cells become flaccid ; <u>turgor pressure</u> is reduced ; [4]

5. (a) Add ethanol and mix ; pour ethanol into water and look for white cloudy appearance ; [2]

(b) (i) To give time for all the solutions to come to the desired temperature ; [1]

(ii) Idea that it is not possible to determine a more precise end-point ; [1]

(iii) Lipase broke down fats to fatty acids (and glycerol) ; fatty acids lower the pH ; [2]

(iv) Kinetic energy of enzyme and substrate molecules lower at 20 °C than at 40 °C ; less frequent collisions (between enzyme and substrate) ; [2]

(v) *Any two of:* Enzyme molecules lost their shape ; <u>denatured</u> ; substrate/fat molecules, no longer fit into active site ; [2]

(vi) Repeat the experiment ; using temperatures on either side of 40 °C ; [2]

2 Nutrition
Plant nutrition

1. Carbon dioxide + water
$\longrightarrow$ glucose + oxygen.

2. So that the oxygen that it gives off can be observed as bubbles, or collected.

3. The rate of photosynthesis increases as temperature increases, until the optimum temperature is reached, after which it decreases.

4. Palisade mesophyll ; spongy mesophyll ; guard cells.

5. To make chlorophyll.

6. $6CO_2 + 6H_2O \longrightarrow C_6H_{12}O_6 + 6O_2$.

7. (a) Starch ; (b) sucrose.

8. Something present in the environment in such short supply that it restricts life processes.

9. Light intensity ; carbon dioxide concentration ; temperature.

10. They allow carbon dioxide to diffuse freely from the stomata to the palisade mesophyll cells.

Human diet and digestion

1. Carbohydrates, fats and proteins.

2. Coronary heart disease ; diabetes.

3. Digestion is needed to produce nutrient molecules that are small enough to be absorbed. Water already has small molecules that do not need to be made any smaller.

4. Salivary glands and pancreas.

5. Mouth and small intestine.

6. Maltose.

7. Small intestine.

8. A disease resulting from very low intake of protein ; the person has a very low body weight, and often a swollen stomach.

9. Pepsin, in the stomach.

10. Neutralises the acidic material entering the small intestine from the stomach so that the enzymes in the small intestine have an optimum pH ; emulsifies fats to make them accessible to lipase.

11. It has villi, which are covered with microvilli ; this increases the surface area, which speeds up the rate of absorption.

Exam-style practice questions

1. (a) 1.46 ; [1]

(b) Carbon dioxide concentration/sodium hydrogencarbonate concentration ; [1]

(c) *Any two of:* Light intensity ; light wavelength ; temperature ; size of plant ; [2]

(d) There was some dissolved carbon dioxide present in the water ; [1]

(e) (i) Light ; [1]
(ii) Carbon dioxide ; water ; [2]
(iii) Carbohydrate/glucose ; [1]

2. (a) $6CO_2 + 6H_2O \longrightarrow C_6H_{12}O_6 + 6O_2$: formulae ; balanced ; [2]

(b) It absorbs energy from light ; which is transferred to chemical energy ; [2]

(c) (i) Increases throughout the whole period ; from 50 g at 20 days to 380 g at 90 days ; mean rate of increase is 4.7 g per day ; [3]

(ii) *Any three of:* more energy available ; more photosynthesis ; light was not a limiting factor ; more carbohydrate synthesised ; [3]

(iii) *Any two of:* Plenty of light already available/light is not a limiting factor ; carbon dioxide concentration/temperature, may be limiting factors ; shading may reduce temperature so plant enzymes can work better ; [2]

(iv) *Any three of:* Used to make cellulose for cell walls ; used to make amino acids for growth ; used to make sucrose to transport to the fruits ; used to make fructose in the fruits ; used for energy for protein synthesis ; [3]

3. (a) (i) Mechanical breaks down large pieces of food to smaller pieces ; chemical breaks down large molecules to smaller molecules ; [2]

(ii) Mouth ; stomach ; [2]

(b) (i) Protease digests protein ; to form amino acids ; [2]

(ii) Gives an acid pH for enzymes ; kills bacteria in food ; [2]

(c) (i) Small intestine/duodenum/ileum ; [1]

(ii) Breaks down maltose ; to glucose ; [2]

(iii) *Any four of:* Mice with version 1 have longer microvilli ; greater surface area ; faster/more efficient, absorption ; (absorption) of digested nutrients/amino acids ; so more amino acids available for protein synthesis ; more maltase so more glucose absorbed ; so more energy for growth ; [4]

3 Transport and immunity
Transport in plants

1. Phloem.

2. Transporting water ; transporting mineral ions ; supporting the plant.

3. See diagrams on page 36.

4. 1 root hair cells, 2 root cortex cells, 3 xylem, 4 leaf mesophyll cells.

5. Loss of water vapour from plant leaves by evaporation of water at the surfaces of the mesophyll cells

Answers

followed by diffusion of water vapour through the stomata.
6. **(a)** Osmosis ;
   (b) active transport or diffusion.
7. It reduces the pressure at the top of the xylem vessels, so water moves up from a region of higher pressure at the base, by mass flow. This is called transpiration pull.
8. Cohesion is a force that holds water molecules together, so the water can all move up in an unbroken column.
9. It increases the kinetic energy of water molecules. This makes liquid water in the cell walls of the mesophyll cells evaporate more quickly. It also makes the water vapour diffuse out of the leaf more quickly.
10. In summer, when leaves are photosynthesising, sucrose is produced there and transported to the roots, so the roots are a sink. In winter, when leaves are not photosynthesising, starch stored in the roots is changed to sucrose and transported to other parts of the plant, so the roots are a source.

Transport in animals
1. They keep blood flowing in the correct direction.
2. Between the right side and the left side.
3. Arteries.
4. ECG ; taking the pulse ; listening to the sound of the valves closing.
5. When the coronary arteries get blocked, so the muscle in the heart wall does not get enough oxygen and cannot contract.
6. Veins.
7. Red blood cells.
8. A double circulation transports oxygenated blood more quickly to the tissues, because the blood goes back to the heart to be pumped out. In a single circulation, the oxygenated blood goes directly from the gills to the tissues, so it travels more slowly.
9. To allow them to expand and recoil as the blood pulses through. This helps them to withstand the high pressure, and it also helps to even out the blood flow.
10. Lymphatic vessels and lymph nodes.

Diseases and immunity
1. A disease-causing organism.
2. Skin ; hairs in the nose.
3. Phagocytosis (engulfing and digesting the pathogen) ; secreting antibodies.

4. Bacteria breed most quickly when it is warm, so this would give time for any harmful bacteria to increase in the food, which could make someone ill when they eat it.
5. They are chemicals secreted by lymphocytes. Each antibody molecule has a shape that is a complementary fit to a particular antigen molecule. The antibodies bind with the antigen, and either destroy it directly, or mark it so that phagocytes will destroy it.
6. In active immunity, a person produces their own antibodies and memory cells, so the immunity lasts a long time. This can be achieved by having the disease, or by vaccination. In passive immunity, a person is provided with antibodies from elsewhere ; there are no memory cells, so the immunity only lasts as long as the donated antibodies last. This can be achieved by a baby feeding on milk from its mother, or by an injection of antibodies.
7. Type 1 diabetes.

Exam-style practice questions
1. **(a) (i)** A aorta *or* B pulmonary vein ;
   (ii) F right ventricle *or* G right atrium ;
   (iii) F right ventricle ; **(iv)** B pulmonary vein ; **(v)** D valve ; **(vi)** G septum ;   [6]
   (b) (i) Coronary arteries ;   [1]
   (ii) *Any two of:* Smoking ; being male ; having genes that predispose you to CHD ; being overweight ; not taking exercise ; eating a diet high in saturated fats or cholesterol ;   [2]
2. **(a)** Rest fingers on an artery, in the neck/in the wrist *or* use a stethoscope *or* use a pulsemeter ; count the number of pulses, per 30 seconds/per minute ;   [2]
   (b) *Any five of:* Muscles contract more ; muscles need more energy ; so more (aerobic) respiration ; so muscles need more oxygen ; (heart beats faster to) move more blood/oxygen to the muscles ; muscles produce more carbon dioxide ; (heart beats faster to) remove more carbon dioxide from the muscles ;   [5]
   (c) *Any four of:* Anaerobic respiration in muscles during exercise ; when not enough oxygen can be supplied ; produces lactic acid ; lactic acid broken down by combining with oxygen ; so extra oxygen required after exercise ; oxygen debt ;   [4]

3. **(a) (i)** *Any two of:* Arteries have thicker walls than veins ; arteries do not have valves but veins do ; arteries have a narrower lumen than veins ;   [2]
   (ii) *Any two of:* (Thicker walls because) arteries carry blood at higher pressure than veins ; (no valves because) high pressure of blood in arteries means that it does not flow backwards/low pressure in veins could allow it to flow backwards ; (narrower lumen because) low pressure of blood in veins needs a wide lumen to reduce resistance to blood flow ;   [2]
   (b) (i) *Any three of:* Overall decrease from 4400000 to 200000 ; decrease of 95.5% ; decrease begins steeply then levels off ; steepest decrease between 1982 and 1987 ; fluctuations between stated years ; (for example 1987 to 1992) ;   [3]
   (ii) *Any three of:* Increase in vaccination ; vaccination increasing rapidly between 1980 and 1990 ; (vaccination increasing rapidly) at the time that cases are decreasing rapidly ; steady high rates of vaccination coincide with steady low rates of cases ;   [3]
   (c) *Any three of:* Immunity develops when a person has produced (a clone of) memory cells ; which can result in the rapid secretion of antibodies against a particular antigen ; antibodies to measles can only bind with measles antigens ; ref. to complementary shape of antibody molecules and antigen molecules ;   [3]

4 Respiration and excretion
Gas exchange in humans
1. Alveoli.
2. Large surface area ; thin surface ; good blood supply ; good ventilation with air.
3. Trachea, bronchus, bronchiole.
4. Inspired air has more oxygen, less carbon dioxide and usually less water vapour.
5. Limewater (or hydrogencarbonate indicator).
6. Becomes faster and deeper.
7. **(a)** Volume increases during breathing in and decreases when breathing out ; **(b)** Pressure

decreases when breathing in and increases when breathing out.

8. External intercostal muscles contract during inspiration and relax during expiration. Internal intercostal muscles relax during inspiration and contract during forced expiration.

9. In the lining of trachea and bronchi. Goblet cells secrete mucus, which traps pathogens and particles. Cilia sweep the mucus to the back of the throat. Between them, they help to keep the lungs clear of pathogens and particles.

Respiration

1. Chemical reactions in cells that use oxygen to break down nutrient molecules to release energy.
2. Glucose + oxygen $\longrightarrow$ carbon dioxide + water.
3. Energy is not produced from nowhere. The energy is already present in the glucose molecules. Respiration simply releases this energy from the glucose.
4. In all body cells.
5. Aerobic respiration uses oxygen, but anaerobic does not ; aerobic respiration produces carbon dioxide and water, but anaerobic respiration produces lactic acid ; aerobic respiration releases more energy from a given quantity of glucose than anaerobic respiration.
6. Anaerobic respiration in humans produces lactic acid, but anaerobic respiration in yeast produces ethanol and carbon dioxide.
7. $C_6H_{12}O_6 + 6O_2 \longrightarrow 6CO_2 + 6H_2O.$
8. $C_6H_{12}O_6 \longrightarrow 2C_2H_5OH + 2CO_2.$
9. In muscles when they are working hard. Muscle contraction requires a lot of energy, and the oxygen supplied by the blood may not be sufficient to support enough aerobic respiration to provide all of this energy.
10. Anaerobic respiration produces lactic acid, which must be broken down. This is done by combining it with oxygen, in the liver. The extra oxygen for this process is supplied by faster breathing (and a faster pulse rate) which continues after exercise until all the lactic acid is broken down.

Excretion

1. In the liver, from excess amino acids.
2. Kidneys.
3. Smaller volume, greater concentration.
4. Ureter is a tube that carries urine from the kidney to the bladder.

Urethra is a tube that carries urine from the bladder to the outside.

5. The removal of the nitrogen-containing part of amino acids to form urea.
6. See diagram on page 59.
7. Concentration is higher in the renal artery (because urea is removed from the blood as it passes through the kidneys).
8. Glomerulus.
9. Water, glucose, urea, mineral salts.
10. Water is reabsorbed from the fluid into the blood, as it passes along the tubule.

Exam-style practice questions

1. (a) (i) *Any two of:* Muscle contraction ; protein synthesis ; cell division ; active transport ; growth ; passage of nerve impulses ; maintenance of constant body temperature ; [2]
   (ii) Glucose + oxygen ; water ; [2]
   (iii) *Any two of:* Releases less energy ; doesn't use oxygen ; produces lactic acid, not carbon dioxide and water ; [2]
   (b) (i) Removal from organisms ; of toxic materials/substances in excess of requirements ; [2]
   (ii) By diffusion ; from the blood into the alveoli ; followed by, breathing out/expiration ; [3]
   (c) (i) Liver ; [1]
   (ii) (Excess) amino acids ; [1]
   (iii) Kidney ; [1]
2. (a) $C_6H_{12}O_6 + 6O_2 \longrightarrow 6CO_2 + 6H_2O$: correct formulae ; balanced ; [2]
   (b) (i) Absorbs carbon dioxide ; so changes in, volume/pressure, are caused only by removal of oxygen from the air ; [2]
   (ii) *Any four of:* Level goes, up on the left hand side/down on the right hand side ; because seeds use oxygen ; in aerobic respiration ; which decreases volume/decreases pressure ; so pressure acting on the liquid in the right hand side of the tube is greater than pressure on the left hand side ; [4]
   (iii) 25.3 and 32.3 ; [1]
   (iv) *Any two of:* Time (before reading taken) ; mass of seeds ; stage of germination of seeds ; type of seeds ; composition of air in the tube at start of experiment ; [2]
   (v) Optimum temperature could be higher than this/she has not tried temperatures above

40 °C ; optimum temperature could be between 30 °C and 40 °C/she has not tried temperatures between 30 °C and 40 °C ; [2]
   (vi) *Any four of:* Movement of fluid increases with temperature ; so rate of respiration increases with temperature ; respiration involves enzymes ; kinetic energy of, enzymes and substrates/reactants, increases with temperature ; more frequent collisions at higher temperatures ; more likely to reach activation energy at higher temperatures ; [4]
3. (a) Diaphragm ; external intercostal ; contract ; volume ; pressure ; [5]
   (b) (i) Maintains a, high concentration of oxygen/low concentration of carbon dioxide, in the alveoli ; maintains a diffusion gradient ; [2]
   (ii) *Any two pairs from:* Large surface area ; so more gases can move across at a given time ; thin surface ; decreases diffusion distance ; good blood supply ; maintains diffusion gradient ; [4]
   (c) (i) A ; [1]
   (ii) *Any two of:* Water is reabsorbed ; into the blood ; urea is not reabsorbed ; [2]

5 Coordination

Nervous control in humans

1. An electrical signal that passes along a neurone.
2. Brain and spinal cord.
3. All of the nervous system apart from the brain and spinal cord ; it is made up of nerves.
4. Sensory, relay, motor.
5. A sensory neurone has a long branch (axon) on either side of its cell body, whereas a motor neurone has only one long branch.
6. Voluntary actions involve the cerebral hemispheres in the brain, but involuntary ones do not. Voluntary actions are not automatic, but can produce different responses to the same stimulus. Voluntary actions are slower.
7. Synapses have neurotransmitter on one side of the synapse only.
8. They are *complementary* in shape, so that the transmitter molecules can fit into the receptor molecules.

Answers

Sense organs

1. Cornea ; pupil ; lens.
2. Retina.
3. Carries nerve impulses from the eye to the brain.
4. A part of the retina where there are no receptor cells, so light falling onto here is not perceived.
5. It gets wider, to let more light into the eye.
6. Circular muscles in the iris.
7. Ciliary muscles.
8. When you focus on a nearby object.
9. The part of the retina where light is focused when you look straight at an object ; it has a high density of cones and no rods.
10. Rods are sensitive to dim light, but cones are only sensitive to bright light. Rods provide black and white vision, but cones provide colour vision.

Hormones in humans

1. A chemical substance, produced by a gland and carried by the blood, which alters the activity of one or more specific target organs.
2. Pancreas.
3. Lower blood glucose concentration.
4. When you are frightened or excited.
5. Increases heart rate, which provides extra oxygen to muscles so that they can respire faster, releasing energy for fight or flight ; increases release of glucose from the liver, providing extra glucose to muscles for the same reason.
6. Nervous control is generally faster and less long-lasting than hormonal control ; nervous control involves electrical impulses along neurones, whereas hormonal control involves chemicals travelling in the blood from glands to target organs.

Homeostasis

1. The maintenance of a constant internal environment.
2. Acts an an insulator, reducing heat loss from the body.
3. Secrete more sweat when body temperature rises too high ; the water in the sweat evaporates, taking heat with it and cooling the skin.
4. A change in a variable is detected, and a response is made that brings the variable back towards normal.
5. Pancreas.
6. Raises blood glucose concentration.
7. Feeling very thirsty ; glucose in the urine ; blurred vision ; feeling very tired between meals.

8. Eating regular small meals ; injecting insulin.

Tropic responses

1. Negative phototropism.
2. It gets more light, so there is more energy available for photosynthesis.
3. A chemical that helps to control plant growth.
4. In the tips of shoots or roots.
5. It makes them elongate.
6. Auxin moves to the side where there is least light, and stimulates the cells there to get longer.

Drugs

1. A substance taken into the body that modifies or affects chemical reactions in the body.
2. Destroying bacteria that are causing an infection.
3. **(a)** Depressant ; **(b)** Stimulant ; **(c)** Depressant.
4. Liver.
5. Tar.
6. Chronic obstructive pulmonary disease ; a condition in which alveolar walls break down, so it is difficult to get enough oxygen into the blood.
7. Fits into receptors at synapses for endorphins ; reduces the production of endorphins.
8. The pattern shown by one variable is matched by the pattern shown by another ; this does not necessarily mean that one is caused by the other.
9. To increase their strength and performance.

Exam-style practice questions

1. **(a) (i)** A spinal cord ; B relay neurone ; [2]
   (ii) C ; [1]
   (iii) *Any two of:* Motor neurone transmits impulses from the spinal cord to an effector, while a sensory neurone transmits impulses from a receptor to the spinal cord ; motor neurone has one long axon, but a sensory neurone has two long axons ; motor neurone's cell body is in the spinal cord, but a sensory neurone's cell body is outside the spinal cord ; [2]
   (b) (i) *Any two of:* A chemical substance produced by a gland ; carried by the blood ; alters the activity of one or more specific target organs ; [2]

   (ii)

Hormone	Gland that secretes it	Function of hormone
insulin	pancreas	reduces blood glucose concentration
testosterone	testes	produces male secondary sexual characteristics
adrenaline	adrenal gland	prepares body for fight or flight, by increasing breathing and pulse rate and dilating pupils

   (1 mark for each correct line) ; [3]
   (c) (i) Positive ; phototropism ; [2]
   (ii) It gets more light ; so it can photosynthesise more ; [2]
2. **(a)** Tip ; accumulates/concentrates/builds up ; darker/shadier/opposite ; elongate/get longer ; [4]
   (b) (i) C/ciliary muscle, contracts ; loosening tension on, B/suspensory ligament ; A/lens becomes, fatter/rounder ; A/lens, bends/refracts, light more ; [4]
   (ii) Rods and cones ; rods are receptive to dimmer light than cones ; rods do not provide colour vision ; [3]
   (c) They do not secrete insulin ; after meal blood glucose concentration rises ; no insulin to lower its concentration ; [3]
3. **(a) (i)** Drug: any substance taken into the body that modifies or affects chemical reactions in the body ; depressant: a drug that slows down nerve impulses and brain activity ; [2]
   (ii) Alcohol is a toxin/damages cells ; liver cells break down alcohol (and are therefore damaged by it) ; [2]
   (b) (i) *Any three of:* Is addictive ; acts as stimulant ; damages blood vessels ; increases risk of developing aneurisms ; increases risk of developing coronary heart disease ; [3]
   (ii) Always a higher number of men with lung cancer than women ; number of men with lung cancer decreases while number of women with lung cancer increases ; comparative figures given for men and women in any stated year ; calculated difference between

figures for men and women in any stated year or over stated period of time ; [4]

(iii) *Any four of:* Idea that lung cancer takes time to develop ; changes in lung cancer rates likely to be affected by changes in smoking patterns well before 1972 ; so we need to see figures for how many men and women were smoking before 1972 ; there is a <u>correlation</u> between the smoking and lung cancer figures for men but not for women ; (in women) correlation does not imply cause and effect ; there could be other factors causing the changes in lung cancer rates ; [4]

6 Reproduction

Asexual and sexual reproduction

1. In asexual there is always only one parent, but in sexual there may be two parents ; in asexual reproduction, all offspring are genetically identical, but in sexual they are genetically dissimilar ; sexual reproduction involves gametes and fertilisation, but asexual does not.
2. For example: budding in *Hydra* ; binary fission in bacteria ; formation of tubers in potatoes ; sucker formation in banana plants.
3. A sex cell, for example a sperm or an egg.
4. The fusion of the nuclei of a male gamete and a female gamete.
5. There is no genetic variation among the offspring, so it is possible that all of the population might be wiped out by an environmental change (for example the arrival of a new disease, or global warming). In plants, there is less chance of dispersal away from the parent plant, so there may be more competition (for example for light) between the offspring.
6. It may take longer than asexual reproduction ; if the organism is rare, it may be difficult for two of them to meet up ; because all of the offspring are genetically different, not all of them may be well-adapted to their environment and may not survive.
7. 4.

Sexual reproduction in plants

1. (a) anther ; (b) stigma ; (c) ovule.
2. Pollen from an insect-pollinated flower is sticky or spiky, rather than smooth, so that it can stick to an insect's body. It is produced in smaller quantities, because less is wasted.
3. The stigma of an insect-pollinated flower is inside the flower, rather than outside, so that insects must brush against it ; the stigma of a wind-pollinated flower is outside the flower, so that the wind can reach it ; the stigma of a wind-pollinated flower is more feathery than an insect-pollinated flower ; this gives it a larger surface area to catch pollen floating on the wind.
4. Suitable temperature ; water ; oxygen.
5. Transfer of pollen grain from the anther of a flower to the stigma of a flower on a different plant of the same species.
6. No need for pollinators.
7. Less genetic variation between offspring.
8. A pollen grain on the stigma grows a tube down the style and into the ovule. The male gamete is a haploid nucleus from the pollen grain. The male gamete travels down the tube and into the ovule, where it meets the female gamete.

Sexual reproduction in humans

1. Produces a fluid in which sperm can swim.
2. The fusion of gamete nuclei.
3. It has a tail (flagellum) ; it has a head containing enzymes ; it is smaller ; it does not contain energy stores ; it does not have a jelly coating.
4. Oviduct.
5. Ovulation ; fertilisation ; implantation.
6. A zygote is the cell that is formed when the nucleus of a male gamete fuses with the nucleus of a female gamete. An embryo is a ball of cells that is formed when the zygote divides repeatedly.
7. Produces female secondary characteristics ; helps to control the menstrual cycle.
8. Condom – placed over penis and prevents semen from entering the female's body. Femidom – placed in vagina, works in similar way to a condom. Diaphragm – placed in vagina at the cervix to prevent sperm swimming to oviduct.
9. HIV.
10. Test people who are at risk of getting HIV, so an infected person knows they are infected and can avoid passing the infection on ; don't share needles for injection ; use condoms during sexual intercourse ; give pregnant women antiretroviral drugs to reduce chance of transmission to the unborn child.
11. It contains enzymes that digest a pathway for the sperm into the egg.
12. Carbon dioxide ; urea.
13. Alcohol ; nicotine.
14. (a) Ovary ; (b) Pituitary gland.
15. Ovary and placenta.
16. It maintains the thick lining of the uterus.
17. AI involves inserting sperm (semen) into the vagina or uterus of a female, and fertilisation takes place inside her body in the usual way. IVF involves extracting eggs from the female and placing them in a dish to which semen is added, so fertilisation takes place in the dish. The resulting embryos are then inserted into the female's uterus.

Exam-style practice questions

1. (a) An infection that is transmitted via body fluids ; through sexual contact ; [2]
   (b) (i) increases ; (apart from a) fall between 2009 and 2010 ; from 100 000 in 2000 to just over 1 000 000 in 2014 ; [3]
   (ii) proportion increases ; from 1 in 6.5 in 2000 to about 1 in 3 in 2014 ; [2]
   (iii) *Any one of:* She may not know that she has HIV ; the drugs may not be available where she lives ; the drugs may be too expensive ; [1]
   (c) Through sexual contact/blood-to-blood contact (for example by sharing needles) ; [1]
   (d) Condom / femidom ; [1]
2. (a) (i) 23 ; [1]
   (ii) *Any two of:* Contains enzymes ; digest a pathway through the outer layers of the egg cell ; to allow fertilisation to take place ; [2]
   (iii) *Any three of:* Provide motility ; mitochondria/C, site of aerobic respiration ; which releases energy that can be used for movement ; flagellum/B, provides propulsion ; [3]
   (b) (i) *Any three of:* Semen collected from male ; semen inserted into, vagina/uterus, of female ; at a suitable time of her reproductive cycle ; fertilisation occurs inside the female's oviducts ; [3]
   (ii) increases then decreases ; from 41 a.u. at time 0 to

Answers

21 a.u. at 150 minutes ; peaks at 51 a.u. at 10 minutes ; [3]

(iii) greater motility ; increases chance of successful fertilisation ; especially if using sperm 10 minutes (or longer) after thawing ; no advantage if using at 10 minutes after thawing ; little advantage if using at 60 minutes after thawing ; [4]

3. (a) (i) The pollen is spiky/the stigma is flat/the stigma is not feathery ; [1]

(ii) Nucleus of pollen grain ; [1]

(iii) *Any three of:* Pollen tube grows into ovule (through micropyle) ; nucleus of pollen grain moves down pollen tube into ovule ; nucleus of pollen grain fuses with nucleus of ovule ; forming a diploid zygote ; [3]

(b) (i) Reference to transfer of pollen from an anther to a stigma ; self-pollination – stigma is on the same plant ; cross-pollination – stigma is on different plant of the same species ; [3]

(ii) Increases genetic variation ; allowing adaptation to changing environment ; [2]

(c) (i) The more neonicotinoid, the less activity/the fewer visits to flowers ; manipulation of data, for example using 10 ppb halves the mean number of visits ; [2]

(ii) Takes time for a fertilised ovule to develop into a seed ; [1]

(iii) *Any three of:* Fruit has developed from an ovary ; ovary may contain several ovules ; seeds only develop if the ovule has been fertilised ; fewer bee visits mean fewer pollen grains left on stigmas ; so fewer ovules are fertilised ; [3]

7 Genetics and selection

Genes and chromosomes

1. A length of DNA that codes for a protein.
2. Nucleus.
3. In the nuclei of their gametes (egg cells and sperm cells).
4. A version of a gene.
5. Four.

6. On ribosomes, in the cytoplasm.
7. The sequence of bases in a DNA molecule (gene).
8. It determines the shape of the protein molecule, which determines its function.
9. mRNA (messenger RNA).
10. (a) two ; (b) one.

Cell division

1. Mitosis and meiosis.
2. Mitosis.
3. Meiosis.
4. Eight.
5. Four.
6. An unspecialised cell, which is able to divide to produce cells that can become specialised.

Inheritance

1.

Genotype	Phenotype
PP	smooth leaves
Pp	smooth leaves
pp	spiky leaves

2. PP.
3. It will make two sorts of gametes, one with genotype G and the other with genotype g.
4. (a) Blue eyes ; (b) bb ; (c) bb ; (d) Bb (because she has brown eyes, so must have a B allele ; and because one of her children has blue eyes, so she must have passed a b allele to them).
5. Parental phenotypes:
   blue eyes   brown eyes
   Parental genotypes:
   bb   Bb
   Gametes:
   all (b)   (B) and (b)
   Offspring genotypes and phenotypes:

   Summary: We would expect a ratio of approximately 1 brown eyes : 1 blue eyes.
6. Test cross.
7. The genotype of a child with blood group O is I°I°, so it has received an I° allele from both parents. So they must both be heterozygous.
   Parental phenotypes:
   blood group A   blood group B
   Parental genotypes:
   IAI°   IBI°
   Gametes:
   (IA) and (I°)   (IB) and (I°)

Offspring genotypes and phenotypes:

	(IB)	(I°)
(IA)	IA IB group AB	IAI° group A
(I°)	IB I° group B	I°I° group O

Summary: The chances of the different blood groups that they might have are 1 group AB : 1 group A : 1 group B : 1 group O.

8. (a) XhY.
   (b) A man's son inherits a Y chromosome from him. The haemophilia gene is on the X chromosome.

Variation and selection

1. For example, human height.
2. Mutation.
3. An inherited feature that helps an organism to survive and reproduce in its environment (or (supplement): the inherited functional features of an organism that increase its fitness).
4. For example: sharp teeth to kill prey ; sandy coloured coat for camouflage.
5. E, A, C, D, B.
6. Genes.
7. A change in the base sequence of DNA.
8. Parental phenotypes:
   carrier   carrier
   Parental genotypes:
   HbA HbS   HbA HbS
   Gametes:
   (HbA) and (HbS)   (HbA) and (HbS)
   Offspring genotypes and phenotypes:

	(HbA)	(HbS)
(HbA)	HbAHbA normal	HbAHbS carrier
(HbS)	HbAHbS carrier	HbSHbS sickle cell anaemia

Summary: The chances of the child having sickle cell anaemia is 1 in 4.
9. The sickle cell allele gives protection against malaria. So a person who is heterozygous, HbAHbS is more likely to survive than someone with the genotype HbAHbA.
10. Air spaces in stems and leaves to allow diffusion of carbon dioxide and oxygen, and also to help the leaves to float so they get more sunlight ; stomata on upper surface of leaf to allow gas exchange.

Biotechnology and genetic engineering

1. It respires anaerobically and produces ethanol. Ethanol can be used as a fuel, or it can be mixed with petrol (gasoline).
2. It produces carbon dioxide, which is trapped in the bread dough and makes it rise.
3. It is an enzyme that digests pectin. It is used for making fruit juice, because it helps to get more juice out of fruit more quickly, and also makes the juice clear instead of cloudy.
4. Protease ; lipase ; amylase.
5. Changing the genetic material of an organism by removing, changing or inserting individual genes.
6. For example: producing rice containing extra vitamin A ; maize that is resistant to insect pests ; soya that is resistant to herbicides.
7. By adding lactase, which breaks down lactose to glucose and galactose.
8. *Penicillium*.
9. To maintain a constant temperature, so that the fungus's enzymes can work correctly.
10. A small circle of DNA in a bacterium.
11. Unpaired lengths of bases at the end of a short length of DNA ; they are produced when DNA is cut by restriction enzymes.

Exam-style practice questions

1. (a) Gene: a length of DNA ; that codes for a protein ; mutation: genetic change ; [3]
   (b) (i) aa ; [1]
   (ii) Parental phenotypes:
       long hair   long hair ;
   Parental genotypes:
       Aa   Aa
   Gametes:
   (A) and (a) (A) and (a) ;
   Offspring genotypes and phenotypes:

	(A)	(a)
(A)	AA long hair	Aa long hair
(a)	Aa long hair	aa short hair

   Genotypes of offspring correct ; phenotypes of offspring correctly matched to genotypes ; [4]
   (c) Long hair is a feature that helps animals to, retain heat/keep warm ; long-haired animals more likely to survive ; (so) long-haired animals more likely to reproduce ;

passing on the long-hair allele to their offspring ; [4]

2. (a) Reproduce quickly ; can make complex molecules ; [2]
   (Note: if you are studying the supplement, you will know other possible reasons as well.)
   (b) (i) Glucose ; ⟶ ethanol + carbon dioxide ; [2]
   (ii) A fuel made from a product of living organisms ; [1]
   (iii) Ethanol ; [1]
   (iv) Making bread ; using carbon dioxide that makes the bread rise ; [2]

3. (a) *Any four of:* Sequence of bases determines the sequence of amino acids in a protein molecule made in the cell ; sequence of amino acids in a protein determines its structure ; the structure of a protein determines its function ; (for example) active site of enzyme must be complementary shape to its substrate ; the proteins made by a, cell/organism, determine its structure and functions ; [4]
   (b) (i) Meiosis ; [1]
   (ii) Copy of each chromosome is made before the cell divides ; one copy goes into each daughter cell ; [2]
   (c) (i) Any specialised cell (for example neurone) and its adaptation (for example long axon) ; [1]
   (ii) Not all genes, used to make proteins/expressed ; different sets of genes expressed produces different structures and functions of cells ; [2]
   (iii) Can divide (by mitosis) ; to produce new cells that can become specialised ; [2]

4. (a) (i) Cut DNA ; to isolate a gene/to open a plasmid ; [2]
   (ii) Joins DNA ; for example to close a plasmid containing an inserted gene ; [2]
   (b) (i) *Any five of:* Choose parents that are exceptionally drought-tolerant ; breed them with each other ; collect seeds and grow into adult plants ; test which ones are most drought-tolerant ; breed most drought-tolerant plants together ; repeat for many generations ; [5]
   (ii) *Any two of:* Less expensive/can be done without specialised laboratory facilities ; may be easier to market a non-

genetically engineered variety ; any other valid point clearly made ; [2]

8 Organisms and environment

Energy flow in ecosystems

1. Water plants ⟶ snails ⟶ snail kites.
2. Energy flow or energy transfer.
3. Water plants.
4.

```
      snail kites ┌──┐
              │  │
         ┌────┴──┴────┐
         │   snails   │
    ┌────┴────────────┴────┐
    │     water plants     │
    └──────────────────────┘
```

5. In the waste products and dead bodies of all of the organisms in the food chain.
6. (a) Light ; (b) chemical energy in food substances.
7. Energy is lost at each transfer because:
   – energy is lost to the environment as heat as a result of respiration in each organism ;
   – not all parts of every organism are eaten by the next organism in the chain ;
   – not all nutrient molecules eaten are digested – some are lost in faeces.
8. The level in a food chain or food web at which an organism feeds.
9. Energy is lost at each step in the chain, so by the time the fifth level is reached, there is rarely enough energy to support a population of organisms feeding at this level.

Nutrient cycles

1. Any organic substance – for example glycogen, protein, fat. (Not cellulose or starch, as these are not found in animals.)
2. Photosynthesis.
3. Carbon that was originally in plants and other organisms, millions of years ago, is released as carbon dioxide.
4. Condensation.
5. (a) Liquid ; (b) vapour or gas.
6. Any protein.
7. Molecules of nitrogen gas are made of two nitrogen atoms combined together with a triple covalent bond. It is very unreactive.
8. Lightning converts nitrogen gas and water in the air to nitrate ions ; nitrogen-fixing bacteria produce ammonium ions.
9. They convert ammonium ions to nitrate ions.
10. Deamination.

Answers

Populations

1. A group of organisms of one species, living in the same area at the same time.
2. Food supply ; predation ; disease.
3. For example: more demand for limited resources such as water or land ; increased risk of conflict ; more pollution, for example more carbon dioxide released into the air ; more habitat destruction ; more disease.
4. A unit containing the community of organisms and their environment, interacting together, for example a decomposing log or lake.
5. A graph of a number of organisms in a population plotted against time ; the first part of the curve is relatively level and is known as the lag phase ; it then climbs steeply in the log or exponential phase ; and then levels off in the stationary phase. It may finally begin to fall in the death phase.
6. Log or exponential phase.
7. **(a)** There are no limiting factors, so birth rate is greater than death rate ; for example there is no competition for food ; **(b)** once numbers reach a certain level, competition for a resource – for example food – will act as a limiting factor and will either increase death rate or decrease birth rate or both.

Human influences on ecosystems

1. Use of chemical fertilisers ; use of herbicides ; use of insecticides ; use of modern machinery.
2. An area containing only a single type of crop plant.
3. Increased areas for crop production, livestock production or housing ; extraction of natural resources ; marine pollution.
4. Stomachs of cattle and sheep ; mud in paddy fields ; decomposing waste at landfill sites.
5. It increases the temperatures on Earth (global warming or climate change), through the enhanced greenhouse effect.
6. One which is produced as rapidly as it is removed from the environment so that it does not run out.

7. Cannot be broken down by decomposers.
8. Burning fossil fuels that contain sulfur (especially coal), releasing sulfur dioxide into the air.
9. Feminisation of aquatic organisms.
10. This reduces the genetic diversity, so the species has less variation that might help it to survive a change in its environment, for example a new disease or global warming.

Exam-style practice questions

1. **(a) (i)** R ; [1]
   (ii) Respiration (by plants) ; [1]
   (iii) Q ; [1]
   (b) (i) Less photosynthesis ; so less carbon dioxide removed from the air ; [2]
   (ii) *Any two of:* Loss of habitats ; extinction of species of plants or animals ; loss of soil ; more flooding ; [2]
   (c) More land can be worked ; by fewer people/in a shorter period of time ; [2]
2. **(a) (i)** All seven species included ; all arrows correct ; [2]

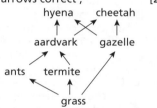

   (ii) Grass ; [1]
   (iii) As chemical energy ; in, nutrients/carbohydrates/fats/proteins ; [2]
   (iv) (Sun)light ; [1]
   (b) (i) *Any two of:* Habitat destruction ; hunting ; climate change ; pollution ; introduced species ; [2]
   (ii) *Any three of:* Captive breeding ; to produce many new individuals ; for eventual return to the wild ; education (of people about the need to conserve the species) ; fund raising ; [3]
3. **(a) (i)** *Any two of:* To make amino acids ; by combination with carbohydrates ; for protein synthesis ; [2]

   (ii) *Any two of:* Energy in lightning ; causes nitrogen to combine with water ; falls to ground in rain ; [2]
   (iii) Bacteria ; produce ammonium ions ; [2]
   (b) *Any five of:* Increased growth of producers/algal bloom ; death of producers ; increased decomposition ; increased aerobic respiration by decomposers ; reduction in dissolved oxygen ; death of organisms requiring dissolved oxygen ; eutrophication ; [5]
4. **(a) (i)**

   | tertiary consumers | |
   secondary consumers
   primary consumers
   producers   10 000 units
   [1]
   (ii) Any number between 5 and 20 ; [1]
   (iii) Not enough energy to support a population of organisms at higher levels ; energy lost at each transfer in the food chain/energy transfer is inefficient ; through respiration/heat lost to the environment/not all organisms eaten ; [3]
   (b) (i) Produced as rapidly as it is removed from the environment ; does not run out ; trees can regrow/be replanted, after being cut down ; [3]
   (ii) *Any five of:* Reducing extinction ; because of habitat loss ; protecting vulnerable environments ; for example reducing soil loss on steep slopes ; for example preventing flooding ; maintaining ecosystem functions ; for example nutrient cycling ; providing resources for humans ; for example food/drugs/fuel/genes ; [5]

Absorption – movement of small food molecules and ions through the wall of the intestine into the blood.

Active immunity – defence against a pathogen by antibody production in the body.

Active transport – the movement of particles through a cell membrane from a region of lower concentration to a region of higher concentration using energy from respiration.

Adaptive feature – the inherited functional features of an organism that increase its fitness.

Aerobic respiration – the chemical reactions in cells that use oxygen to break down nutrient molecules to release energy.

Allele – a version of a gene.

Anaerobic respiration – the chemical reactions in cells that break down nutrient molecules to release energy without using oxygen.

Asexual reproduction – a process resulting in the production of genetically identical offspring from one parent.

Assimilation – movement of digested food molecules into the cells of the body where they are used, becoming part of the cells.

Binomial system – an internationally agreed system in which the scientific name of an organism is made up of two parts showing the genus and species.

Carnivore – an animal that gets its energy by eating other animals.

Catalyst – a substance that increases the rate of a chemical reaction and is not changed by the reaction.

Chemical digestion – breakdown of large, insoluble molecules into small, soluble molecules.

Chromosome – a thread-like structure made of DNA, which carries genetic information in the form of genes.

Community – all of the populations of different species in an ecosystem.

Consumer – an organism that gets its energy by feeding on other organisms.

Cross-pollination – the transfer of pollen grains from the anther of a flower to the stigma of a flower on a different plant of the same species.

Deamination – the removal of the nitrogen-containing part of amino acids to form urea.

Decomposer – an organism that gets its energy from dead or waste organic material.

Diffusion – the net movement of particles from a region of their higher concentration to a lower concentration down a concentration gradient, as a result of their random movement.

Diploid nucleus – a nucleus containing two sets of chromosomes, for example in body cells.

Dominant – an allele that is expressed if it is present.

Drug – a substance taken into the body that modifies or affects chemical reactions in the body.

Ecosystem – a unit containing the community of organisms and their environment, interacting together, for example a decomposing log or a lake.

Egestion – passing out of food that has not been digested or absorbed, as faeces, through the anus.

Enzyme – a protein that functions as a biological catalyst.

Excretion – removal from organisms of the waste products of metabolism (chemical reactions in cells including respiration), toxic materials, and substances in excess of requirements.

Fertilisation – the fusion of gamete nuclei.

Fitness – the probability of an organism surviving and reproducing in the environment in which it is found

Food chain – a diagram showing the transfer of energy from one organism to the next, beginning with a producer.

Food web – a network of interconnected food chains.

Gene – a length of DNA that codes for a protein.

Genetic engineering – changing the genetic material of an organism by removing, changing or inserting individual genes.

Genotype – the genetic make-up of an organism in terms of the alleles present.

Gravitropism – a response in which parts of a plant grow towards or away from gravity.

Growth – a permanent increase in size and dry mass by an increase in cell number or cell size or both.

Haploid nucleus – a nucleus containing a single set of unpaired chromosomes, for example in gametes.

Herbivore – an animal that gets its energy by eating plants.

Heterozygous – having two different alleles of a particular gene.

Homeostasis – the maintenance of a constant internal environment.

Homozygous – having two identical alleles of a particular gene.

Hormone – a chemical substance, produced by a gland and carried by the blood, which alters the activity of one or more specific target organs.

Ingestion – taking substances, for example food and drink, into the body through the mouth.

Inheritance – the transmission of genetic information from generation to generation.

...ctor – something p... in the environment in such sho... supply that it restricts life processes.

Mechanical digestion – breakdown of food into smaller pieces without chemical change to the food molecules.

Meiosis – reduction division in which the chromosome number is halved from diploid to haploid resulting in genetically different cells.

Mitosis – nuclear division giving rise to cells that are genetically identical.

Movement – an action by an organism or part of an organism causing a change of position or place.

Mutation – a change in the base sequence of DNA.

Nutrition – taking in materials for energy, growth and development; plants require light, carbon dioxide, water and ions; animals need organic compounds and ions and usually need water.

Organ – a structure made up of a group of tissues, working together to perform specific functions.

Organ system – a group of organs with related functions working together to perform body functions.

Osmosis – the net movement of water molecules from a region of higher water potential (dilute solution) to a region of lower water potential (concentrated solution) through a partially permeable membrane.

Passive immunity – short-term defence against a pathogen by antibodies acquired from another individual, for example mother to infant.

Pathogen – a disease-causing organism.

Phenotype – the observable features of an organism.

Photosynthesis – the process by which plants manufacture carbohydrates from raw materials using energy from light.

Phototropism – a response in which parts of a plant grow towards or away from the direction from which light is coming.

Pollination – the transfer of pollen grains from the anther to the stigma.

Population – a group of organisms of one species living in the same area at the same time.

Process of adaptation – the process, resulting from natural selection, by which populations become more suited to their environment over many generations.

Producer – an organism that makes its own organic nutrients, usually using energy from sunlight, through photosynthesis.

Recessive – an allele that is only expressed when there is no dominant allele of the gene present.

Reproduction – making more of the same kind of organism.

Respiration – the chemical reactions in cells that break down nutrient molecules and release energy for metabolism.

Self-pollination – the transfer of pollen grains from the anther of a flower to the stigma of the same flower, or a different flower on the same plant.

Sense organs – groups of receptor cells responding to specific stimuli: light, sound, touch, temperature and chemicals.

Sensitivity – the ability to detect or sense stimuli in the internal or external environment and to make appropriate responses.

Sex-linked characteristic – a characteristic in which the gene responsible is located on a sex chromosome and that this makes it more common in one sex than in the other.

Sexual reproduction – a process involving the fusion of the nuclei of two gametes (sex cells) to form a zygote and the production of offspring that are genetically different from each other.

Sexually transmitted infection – an infection that is transmitted via body fluids through sexual contact.

Species – a group of organisms that can reproduce to produce fertile offspring.

Sustainable development – development providing for the needs of an increasing human population without harming the environment.

Sustainable resource – one that is produced as rapidly as it is removed from the environment, so that it does not run out.

Synapse – a junction between two neurones.

Tissue – a group of cells with similar structures, working together to perform a shared function.

Translocation – the movement of sucrose and amino acids in phloem from regions of production (source) to regions of storage or to regions where they are used in respiration or growth (sink).

Transmissible disease – a disease in which the pathogen can be passed from one host to another.

Transpiration – the loss of water vapour from plant leaves by evaporation of water at the surfaces of the mesophyll cells followed by diffusion of water vapour through the stomata.

Trophic level – the position of an organism in a food chain, food web, pyramid of numbers or pyramid of biomass.

Variation – differences between individuals of the same species.